T0318974

Cambridge Elements ≡

Elements in World Englishes
edited by
Edgar W. Schneider
University of Regensburg

THE COGNITIVE FOUNDATION OF POST-COLONIAL ENGLISHES

Construction Grammar as the Cognitive Theory for the Dynamic Model

Thomas Hoffmann
Catholic University Eichstätt-Ingolstadt and Hunan Normal University

CAMBRIDGE
UNIVERSITY PRESS

CAMBRIDGE
UNIVERSITY PRESS

University Printing House, Cambridge CB2 8BS, United Kingdom

One Liberty Plaza, 20th Floor, New York, NY 10006, USA

477 Williamstown Road, Port Melbourne, VIC 3207, Australia

314–321, 3rd Floor, Plot 3, Splendor Forum, Jasola District Centre,
New Delhi – 110025, India

103 Penang Road, #05–06/07, Visioncrest Commercial, Singapore 238467

Cambridge University Press is part of the University of Cambridge.

It furthers the University's mission by disseminating knowledge in the pursuit of
education, learning, and research at the highest international levels of excellence.

www.cambridge.org
Information on this title: www.cambridge.org/9781108829236
DOI: 10.1017/9781108909730

© Thomas Hoffmann 2021

First published 2021

A catalogue record for this publication is available from the British Library.

ISBN 978-1-108-82923-6 Paperback
ISSN 2633-3309 (online)
ISSN 2633-3295 (print)

The Cognitive Foundation of Post-colonial Englishes

Construction Grammar as the Cognitive Theory for the Dynamic Model

Elements in World Englishes

DOI: 10.1017/9781108909730
First published online: November 2021

Thomas Hoffmann
Catholic University Eichstätt-Ingolstadt and Hunan Normal University
Author for correspondence: Thomas Hoffmann, thomas.hoffmann@ku.de

Abstract: Varieties of English are spoken all over the world from Africa to Asia, from Europe to America. In addition to its use as a foreign language, English in many of these countries is a first- or second-language variety that initially arose in a colonial setting. Currently, the most influential sociolinguistic model for the evolution of these 'post-colonial Englishes' is the Dynamic Model. In this Element, I outline how Construction Grammar, the most prominent cognitive syntactic theory, can provide a cognitive foundation for the assumptions made by the Dynamic Model. As I shall argue, Construction Grammar naturally complements the Dynamic Model and, in addition to that, a 'Constructionist Grammar Approach to the Dynamic Model' generates new research questions concerning the productivity of syntactic patterns across Dynamic Model phases.

Keywords: Dynamic Model, post-colonial Englishes, Cognitive Linguistics, Construction Grammar, World Englishes

ISBNs: 9781108829236 (PB), 9781108909730 (OC)
ISSNs: 2633-3309 (online), 2633-3295 (print)

Contents

1 Introduction

Today, English is *the* global language: it is spoken by more than two billion people (Crystal 2008), it is the language of Twitter, TikTok and YouTube, and it is the world's lingua franca of choice. Some of its speakers acquired British English as their mother tongue, many others learnt English as a foreign language. In addition to these, there are many varieties of English that historically arose in colonial settings (so-called 'post-colonial Englishes'). These include first-language (L1) varieties such as American English or Australian English as well as second-language (L2) varieties such as Kenyan English or Hong Kong English. Simply grouping all these varieties under a single umbrella term 'Global English' (Crystal 2003) obviously obscures important differences concerning their synchronic use in the respective countries as well as the diachronic development of these different types of English. Instead, it has become customary to collectively refer to all types of Englishes around the world as 'World Englishes' (Kachru 1992) and various models have been developed as an attempt to categorize and classify the various subtypes of Englishes (for an overview, cf. Buschfeld and Kautzsch 2020; Buschfeld and Schneider 2018; Hundt 2020; Mesthrie and Bhatt 2008; Schneider 2020: 30–8).

In one of the earliest models, Quirk (1985; building on a classification suggested by Strang in the 1970s, cf. Schneider 2020: 31–2) distinguished Englishes based on how most of the speakers in a country acquire the language: in English as a Native Language (ENL) countries such as the UK, the United States, Ireland, Australia or New Zealand it is assumed that people acquire English as their mother tongue. In contrast to this, in countries such as Kenya, India or Malaysia, speakers are claimed to first acquire a local language before learning English as a Second Language (ESL). Nevertheless, due to historical reasons, these ESL varieties play an important internal role in these countries 'e.g. in politics (sometimes as an official or co-official language), education, the media, business life, the legal system, etc.' (Schneider 2020: 31). Finally, there are English as a Foreign Language (EFL) countries where English is predominantly learnt as a foreign language at school and used predominantly for international communication (with hardly any internal functions; cf. Schneider 2020: 31).

Despite its intuitive appeal and conceptual simplicity, the ENL-ESL-EFL model has been criticized for its underlying 'mother tongue' ideology and predominance of ENL varieties (Kachru 1992). As Braj Kachru argued, ESL varieties should not be seen as norm dependent on external EFL models. Instead, he emphasized the independence and practical importance of these varieties in their respective countries. He therefore suggested an alternative model that relabels the three types of varieties as Inner Circle, Outer Circle and Expanding Circle. The advantage of this Three Circle model is that by drawing on the 'growth metaphor' (Schneider 2020: 33) it allows Outer Circle varieties to be seen as naturally developing their own norms and thus being independent of Inner Circle norms.

Both the ENL-ESL-EFL model as well as the Three Circle model have been extremely popular and have spawned important research on World Englishes. At the same time, it has also been pointed out that both models suffer from essentially the same shortcomings: very often the linguistic situation in a country is so complex that it cannot be captured by a simple label. South Africa, for example, has a considerable number of people who speak an ENL variety. Yet, at the same time, a substantial portion of the population has learnt English as an ESL variety. Finally, some groups only learn English at school and hardly use the language in their daily lives, so that it might be an EFL variety for them. Besides, while these varieties used to be ethnically stratified during the apartheid era, their distribution now seems to become more and more dominated by social stratification (Mesthrie 2010).

As Schneider (2003, 2007, 2020) points out, these earlier models suffer from the fact that they 'abstract from complex realities, and . . . fail to reflect the vigorous spread of English and changes of its status in many regions over the last few decades' (Schneider 2020: 34). Moreover, he draws attention to the similar colonial roots of many ENL/Inner Circle and ESL/Outer Circle varieties. American English, Canadian English, Australian English and New Zealand English as well as Ghanaian English, Kenyan English, Indian English and Singaporean English, to name but a few examples, all emerged as part of the British colonial expansion policy starting in the Early Modern period (and ending in the twentieth century). Thus, in contrast to EFL/ Expanding Circles varieties, these so-called post-colonial L1 and L2 varieties are the result of particular contact scenarios in which an English-speaking colonizer/settler (STL) strand went abroad and came into contact with the colonized/Indigenous (IDG) population. Based on this observation, Schneider develops his own model, the Dynamic Model (2003, 2007), whose main claim is that the 'emerging varieties of English in post-colonial contexts have typically followed an underlying, fundamentally uniform evolutionary process caused by the social dynamics between the two parties involved in a colonization process' (Schneider 2020: 34). In other words, the Dynamic Model predicts that similar historical, political, psychological and (socio)linguistic factors are at work in all colonial contact situations and 'that some synchronically observable differences between such [post-colonial] varieties may be regarded as consecutive stages in a diachronic process' (Schneider 2003: 242).

By focusing on the contact dynamics in colonial settings, Schneider obviously not only provides a model for ENL/Inner Circle and ESL/Outer Circle varieties, but also for contact varieties such as English-based pidgins and creoles. As a result of its far-reaching claims and predictions, the Dynamic Model is a powerful, multi-factorial model of the evolution of Englishes that has attracted considerable scholarly attention and interest (cf., e.g., Buschfeld and Kautzsch 2017; Buschfeld et al. 2014; Evans 2009; Mukherjee 2007; Mukherjee and Gries 2009; Thusat et al. 2009; Weston 2011). Yet, as the above shows, the Dynamic Model is essentially a sociolinguistic model, in that linguistic changes are seen to mostly arise from forces related to identity-construction. Recently, Hoffmann (2014, 2019) offered a cognitive, Construction Grammar perspective to this sociolinguistic approach, outlining how the various phases of the Dynamic Model should correlate with an increasing schematization of constructions. Construction Grammar (Croft 2001; Goldberg 2006, 2019; Hilpert 2019; Hoffmann 2017a, 2017b; Hoffmann and Trousdale 2013) is a cognitive theory of language that over the last thirty years has received considerable support from L1 acquisition (cf. Diessel 2013), L2 acquisition (cf. Ellis 2013), psycho- as well as neuro-linguistics studies (cf. Bencini 2013; Pulvermüller, Cappelle and Shtyrov 2013). Its main tenet is that 'constructions', that is, arbitrary form–meaning pairings, are not only a useful concept for the description of words, but that all levels of grammatical description (from morphology to abstract syntactic phenomena such as the passive construction) involve such conventionalized form–meaning pairings (see Section 2.1).

The present Element offers a 'Constructionist Grammar Approach to the Dynamic Model' (CxG-DM). It illustrates how Construction Grammar naturally complements the Dynamic Model and how such an approach also generates new research questions. It shows how the evolutionary stage of a variety can be predicted to correlate with the productivity of constructional schemata and how variety-specific constructional patterns emerge in the different varieties. Section 2 will provide a concise introduction to Construction Grammar (CxG) and give an overview of the Dynamic Model (DM). In addition to this, it will detail how insights from Construction Grammar add a cognitive perspective to the sociolinguistic model (CxG-DM). Section 3 will then present information on the methodology adopted by the CxG-DM approach and the database used for the empirical studies. Finally, Section 4 will present three CxG-DM sample studies, before Section 5 concludes the Element.

2 The Dynamic Model and Construction Grammar

2.1 Usage-based Construction Grammar

Most syntactic approaches from Generative Grammar (Chomsky 1995, 2001) to traditional grammars (Biber et al. 1999; Quirk et al. 1985) assume a clear-cut division of lexical and grammatical knowledge. On the one hand, they postulate a lexicon which contains a large number of symbols, that is, meaningful words (e.g., *orange* which is a pairing of FORM: /ɒɹɪndʒ/ ↔ MEANING 'orange (a particular type of fruit)'). On the other hand, a limited number of abstract, meaningless syntactic rules are posited which combine words into grammatical sentences. In stark contrast to this, Construction Grammar (Goldberg 2006; Hilpert 2019; Hoffmann 2017a, 2017b, 2022; Hoffmann and Trousdale 2013) rejects this lexicon-syntax dichotomy. Instead, Construction Grammar maintains that there is 'a uniform representation of all grammatical knowledge in the speaker's mind, in the form of . . . constructions' (Croft and Cruse 2004: 255). The basic units of all grammatical knowledge are therefore constructions, which are defined as arbitrary and conventional pairings of form and meaning. Examples of constructions are given in (1)–(4) (employing a fairly informal description of the FORM and MEANING parts; for various different approaches to the representation of constructions, cf. Hoffmann 2017a, 2017b; Hoffmann and Trousdale 2013):

(1)   morpheme construction
      un-V-construction:
      FORM: $[ʌn]_1$-V_2 ↔ MEANING: 'reverse$_1$ V-action$_2$'
      (e.g., *undo, untie, uncover*)

(2)   idiom construction
      FORM: SBJ_1 $SPILL_2$ $[ðə\ biːnz]_3$ ↔ MEANING: 'X$_1$ divulge$_2$ the-information$_3$'
      (modelled on Croft and Cruse 2004: 252)
      (e.g., *He spilled the beans.*, *She has spilled the beans.*, *Their neighbours will spill the beans.*)

(3)   Intransitive Motion construction:
      FORM: SBJ_1 V_2 $OBL_{3\_path/loc}$ ↔ MEANING: 'Theme$_1$ moves-by-manner$_2$ GOAL$_{3\_path/loc}$'
      (e.g., *She ran into the room.*, *The fly buzzed out of the window.*, *They strolled along the road.*)

(4)   Transitive construction:
      FORM: SBJ_1 V_2 OBJ_3 ↔ MEANING: 'Agent$_1$ exerts-force-onto$_2$ Patient$_3$'
      (e.g., *She kissed him.*, *He sang a song.*, *They smashed a wall.*)

Just like the word *apple*, all the constructions in (1)–(4) are symbols – pairings of FORM and MEANING (with the bidirectional arrow '↔' expressing the arbitrary, symbolic relationship between the two poles): (2) has a FORM pole [X_1 SPILL$_2$ [ðə bi:nz]$_3$]) as well as a MEANING pole ('X_1 divulge$_2$ the-information$_3$'). In contrast to word constructions, whose FORM pole is completely phonologically fixed, other constructions can contain schematic slots, that is, positions that can productively be filled by various elements. While the *the beans* part in (2) is phonologically fixed (you cannot, e.g., say *He spilled the **peas*** with the intended idiomatic meaning), various noun phrases (NPs) can appear in the subject X slot (see the examples in (2)). Moreover, the verb in (2) has to be the lexeme construction SPILL (which, however, is at least partly flexible in that it can be realized by various tensed verb forms such as *spilled* or *will spill*). Similarly, a morpheme construction such as the *un*-V-construction comprises fixed as well as schematic positions (1). The Intransitive Motion construction in (3), on the other hand, is a completely schematic construction that only contains slots for the theme SBJ, the verb V, and the path-/ location-goal OBL (and thus licenses diverse structures such as the ones given in (3)). Similarly, the Transitive construction, which encodes a force-dynamic event of an agent exerting (concrete or abstract) force onto a patient (Croft 2012: 282), is also fully schematic (with slots for agent, patient as well as the verbal predicate that specifies the type of force-dynamic event).

Recently, Construction Grammar has received considerable empirical support from psycholinguistics (inter alia Bencini 2013; Bencini and Goldberg 2000; Bencini and Valian 2008; Chang 2002; Chang, Bock and Goldberg 2003; Chang et al. 2000; Dominey and Hoen 2006; Konopka and Bock 2008; Perek 2015; Wardlow Lane and Ferreira 2010) as well as neurolinguistics (Cappelle, Shtyrov and Pulvermüller 2010; Pulvermüller 1993, 2003, 2010; Pulvermüller and Knoblauch 2009; Pulvermüller, Shtyrov and Cappelle 2013).

Bencini and Goldberg (2000) conducted an experiment in which they crossed four verbs (*throw, get, slice* and *take*) with four different constructions (examples from Bencini and Goldberg 2000: 650):

- the Transitive construction (see (4) above):
  FORM: SBJ$_1$ V$_2$ OBJ$_3$ ↔ MEANING: 'Agent$_1$ exerts-force-onto$_2$ Patient$_3$' (e.g., *Anita$_1$ threw$_2$ [the hammer]$_3$.*, *Anita$_1$ sliced$_2$ [the bread]$_3$.*)
- the Ditransitive construction:
  FORM: SBJ$_1$ V$_2$ OBJ$_3$ OBJ$_4$ ↔ MEANING: 'Agent$_1$ by V-ing$_2$ causes Recipient$_3$ to receive Theme$_4$' (e.g., *Chris$_1$ threw$_2$ Linda$_3$ [the pen]$_4$.*, *Jennifer$_1$ sliced$_2$ Terry$_3$ [an apple]$_4$*).
- the Caused Motion construction:
  FORM: SBJ$_1$ V$_2$ OBJ$_3$ OBL$_4$ ↔ MEANING: 'Agent$_1$ by V-ing$_2$ causes Theme$_3$ to move to Goal$_4$' (e.g., *Pat$_1$ threw$_2$ [the keys]$_3$ [onto the roof]$_4$.*, *Meg$_1$ sliced$_2$ [the ham]$_3$ [onto the plate]$_4$.*)

- the Resultative construction:
  FORM: SBJ$_1$ V$_2$ OBJ$_3$ OBL$_4$ ↔ MEANING: 'Agent$_1$ by V-ing$_2$ causes
  Patient$_3$ to become Result-Goal$_4$' (e.g., *Lyn$_1$ threw$_2$ [the box]$_3$ apart$_4$.,
  Nancy$_1$ sliced$_2$ [the tire]$_3$ open$_4$.*)

The sixteen stimuli (four verbs crossed with four constructions) were then shuffled and presented to subjects who were asked to sort the sentences into four piles 'based on the overall meaning of the sentence, so that sentences that were thought to be closer in meaning were placed in the same pile' (Bencini and Goldberg 2000: 644). Subjects could, consequently, either choose to sort the sentences by verbs (e.g., putting all *threw*-examples into one pile and all *sliced*-examples into another one) or by construction (grouping all Transitive constructions in one pile and all Ditransitive constructions in another). As the results showed, even though subjects were not explicitly instructed to do so, they predominantly sorted the sentences by constructions (Bencini and Goldberg 2000: 644–7). Gries and Wulff replicated this sorting study with German learners of English and found that they also 'exhibited a strong tendency towards a constructional sorting style' (2005: 192).

Priming studies also provide evidence for the existence of constructions: Johnson and Goldberg (2013) presented subjects with an argument structure construction containing nonsense verbs such as the ditransitive *He daxed her the norp* (2013: 1443). After that, subjects had to carry out a lexical decision task (decide whether an item they saw was a 'word' or 'non-word'). The items in the experiment included verbs that are semantically related (e.g., *gave*, *handed* and *transferred*), but differ in their association with an argument structure construction: *gave* is used highly frequently in the Ditransitive construction (*She gave him the money*), *handed* appears less frequently in the construction (*She handed him the money*), and *transferred* is not really associated with the construction (cf. *She transferred him the money* vs the preferred Cause Motion version *She transferred the money to him*). As Johnson and Goldberg (2013) showed, the argument structure construction with the nonsense verb strongly primed the verbs that were associated with the construction, but not the non-associated ones: *gave* and *handed* were identified as 'words' significantly faster than *transferred* after subjects had seen *He daxed her the norp*. Since *dax* is a nonsense verb, what primed *gave* and *handed* in this case was the abstract meaning of the Ditransitive construction with which they are regularly used.

Allen et al. (2012), furthermore, found neurolinguistic support for the existence of abstract constructional templates: in their experiment, subjects were presented with the same lexical material, either embedded in the Ditransitive construction (e.g., *James e-mailed Matt a document*) or the Caused Motion construction (e.g., *James e-mailed a document to Matt*). As the statistical analysis of their fMRI data revealed, despite using the same nouns and verbs, the different argument structure constructions were associated with distinct activation patterns in the left hemisphere (left anterior Brodmann area 22 as well as Brodmann area 47). As these areas are implicated in the semantic processing of language, these findings offer further support for the cognitive reality of meaningful abstract constructional patterns (see also Goldberg 2019: 33–4).

In addition to this, there is a large emerging body of empirical work on L1 acquisition (inter alia Brooks and Tomasello 1999a, 1999b; Brooks et al. 1999; Clark 1987; Dąbrowska 2000; Dąbrowska and Lieven 2005; Dąbrowska, Rowland and Theakston 2009; Diessel 2004, 2005, 2009, 2013; Rowland 2007; Rowland and Pine 2000; Tomasello 1999, 2003; Tomasello and Brooks 1998) as well as L2 acquisition (inter alia Ellis 2002, 2003, 2006, 2013; Gries and Wulff 2005, 2009; McDonough 2006; McDonough and Mackey 2006; McDonough and Trofimovich 2008; Wulff et al. 2009) that provide further evidence that Construction Grammar is a realistic and successful model of mental grammar.

There are many different Construction Grammar approaches (see Hoffmann 2017b), but the ones that have received most empirical support so far are all usage-based (Barlow and Kemmer 2000; Bybee 2006, 2010, 2013): this approach takes seriously the role that authentic input plays for the emergence of speakers' mental grammars (see also Barðdal 2008, 2011; Croft 2001). As Croft and Barðdal have pointed out, the input to which speakers are exposed does not always automatically lead to maximally abstract mental generalizations (such as (3) and (4) above), but might only lead to partly schematic and partly substantive generalizations. Moreover, mainstream usage-based approaches assume that mental representations are stored in taxonomic networks (cf. Croft and Cruse 2004: 262–5; Goldberg 2006: 215): speakers first encounter specific, substantive instances of a construction (e.g., *He kissed John*), which are stored in an exemplar-based fashion. Only structures with a high type frequency, that is, those that have been encountered with many different lexicalizations *(She kissed John / Bill cut the bread / Barbara closed the door . . .)*, all of which share a common meaning (of an agent exerting force onto a patient), contribute to the entrenchment of a more abstract construction such as (4) above (cf. Goldberg 2006: 39, 98–101; see also Bybee 1985, 1995; Croft and Cruse 2004: 308–13).

From a usage-based perspective, type and token frequency thus interact to create a mental construction network that ranges from more specific,

substantive constructions at the bottom to more and more schematic constructions at the top. Take, for instance, the partial construction network for the
Ditransitive construction (FORM: $SBJ_1\ V_4\ OBJ_2\ OBJ_3 \leftrightarrow$ MEANING: 'Agent$_1$
causes Recipient$_2$ to receive Patient$_3$ by V_4-ing') provided in Figure 1 (for
further details, see Hoffmann 2017b).

At the bottom of Figure 1, we see specific utterances (so-called 'constructs')
such as *She refused him a kiss*, which a speaker will be exposed to. If such
a construct has a high token frequency it can become entrenched as a fully
substantive 'micro-construction' in the long-term memory. If, however, different types of the pattern (e.g., *They refused him the answer, John refused his
parents entry to his room*) are encountered, schematization will lead to the
entrenchment of a slightly more abstract constructional template (a so-called
'meso-construction', cf. the REFUSE.Verb-Specific construction in Figure 1).
Similarly, input such as *He denied him the answer* Or *She denied him entry to
her room*, will lead to a DENY.Verb-Specific meso-construction. After that,
schematization can continue further since both the REFUSE.Verb-Specific
construction and the DENY.Verb-Specific construction share important
FORM and MEANING similarities, which are captured by the slightly more
abstract REFUSE.Verb-Class-Specific Ditransitive meso-construction in
Figure 1 (whose central sense is 'Agent$_1$ causes Recipient$_2$ **not** to receive
Patient$_3$ by V_4-ing'). Finally, the existence of other ditransitive verb-class-
specific constructions (such as GIVING.Verb-Class-Specific Ditransitive construction, which licenses constructs such as *She passed him the salt* Or *They
served him dinner*, or the BALL.MOT.Verb-Class-Specific Ditransitive construction such as *He threw her the ball* Or *They tossed him a towel*) might give
rise to a maximally abstract ditransitive 'macro-construction' (FORM: $SBJ_1\ V_4$
$OBJ_2\ OBJ_3 \leftrightarrow$ MEANING: 'Agent$_1$ causes Recipient$_2$ to receive Patient$_3$ by V_4
-ing'). Note, from a usage-based perspective, the existence of such maximally
abstract constructions is an empirical issue: if such abstract ditransitive constructions existed, it should be possible to use verbs like *pass* or *refuse* in any of
the available sub-schemas and the resulting overall meaning should be provided
by the schematic construction. Yet, as Croft (2012: 377) points out, *pass* in the
Ditransitive construction cannot mean 'X passes Y to receive Z by instantan-
eous ballistic motion' nor can *refuse* be made to mean 'X refuses Y to receive
Z (and Y successfully receives Z)'. Instead of assuming a maximally taxonomic
superordinate Ditransitive construction (sometimes referred to as a 'macro-
constructional level'), it might therefore instead be sufficient for speakers to
abstract to an intermediate schematic verb-class-specific level (also known as
'meso-constructional level'). The right level of granularity of constructional
schematicity, consequently, remains a central issue in all Construction Grammar

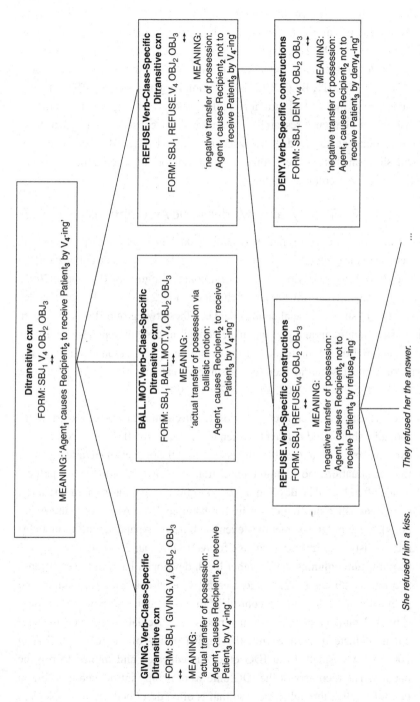

Figure 1 Partial construction network for the Ditransitive construction (Hoffmann 2017b: 314)

approaches (for details, see Hoffmann 2017b). Previous research has shown, for instance, that the *Way* construction (e.g., *He drunk his way through town*) is fairly productive and can combine with a great number of different verbs (Goldberg 1995: 199–218), while the Resultative construction (e.g., *He wiped the table clean*) is lexically much more constrained and thus much less productive (Boas 2005, 2011; Boas 2013: 237–8; Goldberg and Jackendoff 2004).

Concerning the mental grammars of speakers, an important insight of Construction Grammar research is, therefore, that constructional generalizations can occur at varying degrees of schematicity (Hilpert 2013: 201–3) and, as I will show in this Element, this point has important repercussions for the evolution of post-colonial Englishes.

2.2 The Dynamic Model: Basic Assumptions

As mentioned in Section 1, in the Dynamic Model the roots of any post-colonial variety lie in the contact situation of a colonizer STL strand and a colonized IDG strand. In line with previous research on contact linguistics (Mufwene 2001; Thomason 2001; Winford 2003; cf. Schneider 2007: 21–2), the Dynamic Model assumes that stronger social contact between these two groups leads to greater linguistic interaction and that language contact in general depends heavily on social and political conditions. For the evolution of post-colonial varieties, the type of contact scenario therefore assumes great importance (cf. Mufwene 2001, 2004; Schneider 2007: 24–5, 2020: 49–52):

- The earliest types of contact scenarios, **trade colonies**, were characterized by sporadic, short-lived contact between the STL and the IDG strand during the exchange of goods and commodities (which at the time even included slaves). In these situations, no common lingua franca was available to the two parties, which often led to the development of pidgins. Once long-term trading posts were established in a region (as in, for example, West Africa or many Asian ports), these pidgins sometimes even 'stabilized, expanded, and in fact c[a] me to exist . . . as distinct language forms' (Schneider 2020: 49).
- **Exploitation colonies**, on the other hand, developed later, in the eighteenth and nineteenth centuries. In these cases, foreign countries came under the political and administrative control of European colonial powers, but only a limited number of STL administrators were actually deployed to these colonies. Instead, in line with the British policy of indirect rule (Lange 2004: 908), a small, local IDG elite was educated and trained to run the country. The members of the IDG elite were mainly introduced to a formal type of English through education that is often described as 'an elitist class marker, formal and influenced by written styles to the point of being

"bookish"' (Schneider 2001: 46). It is this type of formal English[1] that was the source of many present-day African and Asian ESL varieties.

- In contrast to exploitation colonies, **settlement colonies** were created by the large-scale migration and settlement of English-speaking STLs. Settlement colonies include the United States, Canada, Australia and New Zealand, and linguistically are characterized by two processes (Schneider 2020: 50). First, the STL strand usually contained people from many different English dialect backgrounds. Due to extensive dialect contact and mutual accommodation in the colonies, the dialect differences between the various STL speakers tended to be minimized and a new common dialect arose via this process of koinéization (Trudgill 2004). Second, the IDG group in these colonies was suddenly faced with a dominant superstrate English-speaking community, which often required 'them to become bilingual or even undergo language shift' (Schneider 2020: 51).
- Finally, **plantation colonies** also exhibited a considerable number of English STLs, but also involved another non-IDG group that was brought to these colonies: these included either slaves, which were relocated by force (mostly from Africa) or indentured labourers (from e.g., India). Plantation colonies therefore consisted of a substantive number of STL English speakers, an IDG group (which in some cases was marginalized or even exterminated as on most Caribbean islands; cf. Schneider 2007: 61) as well as a non-IDG group, which usually constituted the numerical majority and comprised the largest number of speakers from various language backgrounds. The multilingual situation of the slaves in these colonies 'typically [led] to strong contact-induced restructuring and possibly to *creolization*' (Schneider 2007: 60).

Yet, while Schneider acknowledges the importance of the local ecology of the initial STL-IDG contact situation (together with the effect of well-known ecological constraints, including the demographic size of groups or the influential 'founder effect' of the earliest members of a new community; Mufwene 2001; cf. Schneider 2007: 25, 110–12), he also points out that the differentiation of the four colony types is 'important mostly for the early phases of settlement' (Schneider 2007: 25):

> How or why two groups were brought together and what their relationship was like in the early phases of contact turns out to be less important in the long run than the recognition that once the settler group stays for good they will have to get along together, for better or for worse. This insight forces all the

---

[1] Toward the end of the British Empire in the post–World War II era, this variety of English was taught more widely and made available to larger chapters of the population (cf. Schneider 2020: 50).

parties involved in a contact setting to reconsider and rewrite their percep-
tions of themselves, their social identities – a process with direct linguistic
consequences. (Schneider 2007: 25–6)

Thus, Schneider considers 'identity constructions and realignments, and their
symbolic linguistic expressions, [to be] also at the heart of the process of the
emergence of PCEs [post-colonial Englishes]' (2007: 28). Consequently, the
Dynamic Model predicts that the evolutionary path that a post-colonial variety
takes crucially depends on the identity (re-)writings of both the STL and the
IDG strands. Moreover, the model assumes that the evolution of post-colonial
Englishes proceeds along five successive phases (Foundation, Exonormative
Stabilization, Nativization, Endonormative Stabilization and Differentiation),
each of which is characterized by a unilateral implication of the following four
sets of conditions (the following list is taken from Schneider 2020: 34–8):

- the political history of a country is reflected in
- the identity re-writings of the groups involved in these processes, which, in
turn, determine
- the sociolinguistic conditions of language contact, linguistic usage and language attitudes; and these affect
- the linguistic developments and structural changes in the varieties evolving.

The Dynamic Model (cf. also Schneider 2007: 31–2) assumes that extralin-
guistic factors, such as historical or political events, can lead to situations which
require the STL and the IDG strands to re-interpret their identity construction.
This, in turn, affects the sociolinguistic factors of the contact situation (such as
'conditions of language contact, language use, and language attitudes'
Schneider 2007: 31).

This causal interaction of social and linguistic factors is supposed to be at
work in all of the five developmental stages of the Dynamic Model, as Figure 2
shows.

While not all varieties will go through all of the five stages in Figure 2, the
Dynamic Model predicts that all the four social and linguistic sets of conditions
play a crucial role at each stage.

2.3 Constructions in the Dynamic Model

Next, I will illustrate how the CxG-DM brings an important cognitive perspective
to the Dynamic Model and which role constructions play during its various stages.
For this, I will particularly focus on the linguistic developments and structural
effects at each of the five characteristic phases of the model (Foundation,
Exonormative Stabilization, Nativization, Endonormative Stabilization and

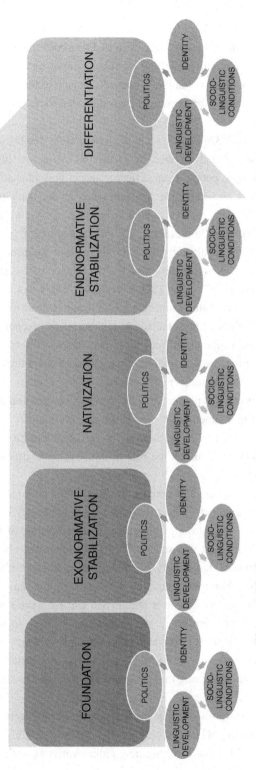

Figure 2 The five consecutive development stages of the Dynamic Model (Hoffmann 2019: 192)

Differentiation; see also Buschfeld et al. 2014). As I shall argue, such a re-interpretation of the linguistic innovations of PCEs as constructional innovation is not only merely a case of re-labelling existing analyses. Instead, the constructionist approach provides a cognitively plausible account of the linguistic evolution of PCEs and, on top of that, also raises new questions for future studies within the Dynamic Model.

As Schneider (2007: 33–6) points out, the first phase of the Dynamic Model, Foundation, is mainly characterized by settler (STL)-internal linguistic processes. In the colonies, people from different accent and dialect backgrounds had to interact and accommodate to each other in the settlements, which ultimately led to 'dialect contact, dialect mixture and new-dialect formation' (Trudgill 2004: 13). This 'koinézation', the emergence of a single, middle-of-the-road variety, is the result of mutual accommodation and processes such as 'levelling, "focusing", simplification and the occurrence of . . . grammatically intermediate "interdialect" forms' (Schneider 2007: 35). From a Construction Grammar point of view, dialect contact involves the interaction of speakers with similar, but nevertheless (slightly) different constructional taxonomic networks. As expected in these situations, infrequent constructions of only a small number of speakers will often be lost, while form–meaning mappings that can be understood by a large number of speakers will become more strongly entrenched. The precise dynamics of constructional koinézation are, however, not examined in this Element, as it mainly focuses on linguistic developments due to inter-group contact. Nevertheless, future constructionist research will obviously also have to focus on the role of constructional networks in inter-group koinézation.

In contrast to intra-group STL contact, the Foundation phase is characterized by relatively limited (socio-)linguistic contact between the newly arrived STL strand and the local IDG group. Consequently, the influence of the IDG languages on STL English at this stage is limited to toponymic borrowings. In constructionist terms, STL speakers thus add a limited number of fully substantive constructions to their mental construction that are highly salient in the local context ('anybody who is new to a region will ask for names of places and landmarks and accept them as . . . the names which these localities simply "have"'; Schneider 2007: 36). Consequently, these place names will also have a high token frequency which will further facilitate their entrenchment. Finally, due to their referential meaning these mappings of form and meaning are fairly easily learnt by STL speakers.

The most interesting linguistic phenomena at this stage occur in trade colonies. There the limited STL-IDG contact often leads to pidginization (cf. e.g., Lefebvre 2004: 7–23). The resulting new pidgin varieties in these situations derive some of their properties from the superstrate STL language (mostly lexical items) and some from the substrate IDG languages (mostly phonological as well as syntactic features). On top of that, however, pidgins also exhibit several features which can neither be found in the super- nor the substrate-input languages and which, therefore, must be the result of the specific language contact characterizing this type of situation or possibly universal contact characteristics (e.g., Lefebvre 2004: 23–8). From a Construction Grammar perspective, it is particularly these latter types of characteristics that are of great interest: almost all constructionist approaches deny the existence of an innate language capacity (in stark contrast to Universal Grammar (Chomsky 1995, 2001) or Language Bioprogram Hypothesis (Bickerton 1981, 1984, 2008) approaches). Instead, general cognitive processes (such as categorization and cross-modal association, as well as iconicity, metaphor, metonymy and processing constraints; Bybee 2010, 2013) are supposed to be responsible for cross-linguistic similarities and typological generalizations. Consequently, all of the syntactic features prototypically associated with pidgins (such as a strong preference for analytic structures or a smaller number of clausal patterns; cf., e.g., Winford 2003: 276) must be explainable with these cognitive principles and processes. A full-scale discussion of a constructionist analysis of pidginization is beyond the scope of the present Element. Nevertheless, from a Construction Grammar point of view the prevalence of analytic structures in pidgins must be interpreted as a cognitive preference for substantive form–meaning pairings (for further support of this view, cf. Baker and Huber 2000: 853; Velupillai 2015). Take the following examples from Cameroon Pidgin English (taken from Mesthrie et al. 2000: 271) as an example:

(5)   a. This small swine he **been go** for market
            'This little piggy **went** to the market'

         b. This small swine he **been stay** for house
            'This little piggy **stayed** home'

The two lines in (5) are from the Cameroon Pidgin English version of the well-known *This little piggy* nursery rhyme. As you can see, in contrast to the synthetic British English past tense verbs *stayed* and the irregular verb *went*, Cameroon Pidgin English uses an analytic *been* + V_{base} pattern to express past tense:

(6)   Simple Past construction (Cameroon Pidgin English)
         FORM: PHONOLOGY: / bin_1 X_2 /
                          MORPHOSYNTAX: $been_1$ V_{base2}
         ↔
         MEANING: SEMANTICS: 'PAST$_1$(V$_2$)'

As the template in (6) shows, the construction has an analytic structure: the invariant element *been* marks the past tense reference, while the second slot specifies the event encoded by the verbal predicate. From a Construction Grammar perspective, the prevalence of analytic grammatical constructions shown in (6) must be interpreted as a cognitive preference for pairings of one form-one meaning in pidgins (i.e., a tendency for isomorphism; Givón 1985; Haiman 1980, 1983, 1985; Schneider 2012: 75; Steger and Schneider 2012). This view receives at least some support from language acquisition: during the earliest stages of language acquisition, children employ holophrase constructions (i.e., linguistic symbols such as *Birdie!* or *Lemme-see!*), which they treat as unanalysed chunks to express their intentions with respect to a specific scenario (cf. Diessel 2013; Tomasello 2006: 23). In the next stage, however, around the age of eighteen months, children start to tweak these utterance-level constructions by adding a single substantive construction or by inserting a substantive form–meaning pairing into the former holophrase structure (Tomasello 2003: 308–9). The earliest stages of creative language use thus involve analytic substantive constructions, and it is therefore no surprise that these types of constructions also play a crucial role during the birth of new languages during pidginization.

In addition to this, domain-general cognitive processes (such as iconicity, metaphor or metonymy) play a great role in how these analytic constructions are used to express concepts for which pidgin speakers have no available stored construction (examples in (7), from Mesthrie et al. 2000: 282):

(7) a. gras   bilong   hed
        grass   belong   head
        'hair'

     b. wara   bilong   skin
        water   belong   skin
        'sweat'

     c. pinga   bilong   lek
        finger belong   leg
        'toe'

Example (7) illustrates how an 'N belong N' construction is used to encode concepts such as *hair*, *sweat* and *toe*. Similar to what we find in L1 acquisition, the construction can be seen in a verb-island construction that has slots for two nouns:

(8) N-*bilong*-N construction (Cameroon Pidgin English)
     FORM: PHONOLOGY: / X_1 bilɔŋ$_2$ Y_3 /
                        MORPHOSYNTAX: N_1 *bilong$_2$* N_3
        ↔

MEANING: SEMANTICS: 'THING$_4$ with METONYMY RELATION$_2$ to THING$_3$ and METAPHOR RELATION$_2$ to THING$_1$'

As the template in (8) shows, the construction is intended to denote a THING$_3$ that is not explicitly mentioned. So how do people know what the speaker meant? Well, the second N$_3$ slot gives them an entity that is metonymically related to the concept they want to express (*head, skin, leg*) and the first N$_1$ slot provides a THING$_1$ that is metaphorically similar to it (*gras, water, finger*). Drawing on the construction in (8) and using domain-general cognitive processes, hearers can thus successfully infer the intended meaning ('finger belong leg' → toe).

Focusing again on the linguistic effects of the STL-IDG interaction during the evolution of PCEs, the next phase of the Dynamic Model is Exonormative Stabilization. During this phase, STL-IDG contact is still superficial but strong enough to result in 'numerous borrowings from indigenous languages ... [which largely] designate the local fauna and flora, soon followed by words for cultural terms, customs and objects found to be peculiar to the indigenous community' (Schneider 2007: 39). The increased contact thus leads to the borrowing of a set of fully substantive, locally salient and very frequent micro-constructions. In contrast to the toponymic constructions of the Foundation phase, these constructions are not referential in meaning but denote sets of objects (cf. Schneider 2007: 39). Nevertheless, these are still straightforward substantive pairings of form and meaning that can easily be added to the taxonomic constructional networks of the STL strand.

In plantation settlements, however, the contact situation during Phase II was considerably different (see Schneider 2007: 62–3). The adstrate of African slaves brought to plantations spoke a wide variety of not necessarily mutually intelligible languages: 'To fulfil their communicative needs as human beings, they were therefore forced to adjust to the new linguistic environment as rapidly and as effectively as possible' (Schneider 2007: 62). The need for a common means of communication in these situations led to structural Nativization, the evolution of English-based creoles ('beginning in phase 1 and certainly in phase 2' Schneider 2007: 62). In contrast to pidgins, creoles are thus used in a wider range of situations and later become the L1 of a second generation of speakers. As a result of being the major means of daily communication, creoles develop more complicated grammatical structures than pidgins. At the same time their grammatical structures also tend to be analytic rather than synthetic (Velupillai 2015). Take the following example from Jamaican Creole (data from Patrick 2008: 614):

(9)   Jamaican Creole

    a. Mi run,   'I ran.'

    b. Mi lov im.   'I love him.'

(10) a. Mi ben ron.   'I had run.'

    b. Mi ben lov im. 'I loved him.'

As (9) shows, in Jamaican Creole an unmarked stative verb such as *love* gets a present tense interpretation, while an activity verb such as *run* is interpreted as past tense. The structure *ben* + V is then used to express a PAST-BEFORE reading. Consequently, (10a) *ben ron* means 'had run' and (10b) *ben lov* means 'loved'.

(11)   Simple Past-before construction (Jamaican Creole)
    FORM: PHONOLOGY: / ben_1 X_2 /
                    MORPHOSYNTAX: ben_1 V_{base2}
    ↔
    MEANING: SEMANTICS: 'PAST-BEFORE$_1$(V_2)'

A template for this Simple Past-before construction can be seen in (11). Similar to the Cameroon Pidgin English construction (6), (11) is analytic in that the PAST-BEFORE meaning is encoded by a single substantive element (*ben$_1$*). At the same time, we have already seen that the precise interpretation of (11) will depend on the verbal aspect of the predicate (something that the template glosses over). Moreover, creoles are also more complex since tense constructions interact with aspect constructions (data from Patrick 2008: 614):

(12) a. Mi a ron.   'I am running.'

    b. Mi ben a ron. 'I was running.'

The above examples illustrate that the Jamaican Creole verb phrase also includes a progressive construction that can be captured by a template of FORM: a_1 + V_{base2} ↔ ONGOING$_1$ (V_2). (As (12b) illustrates, the template in (11) would have to be modified in a way that the tense marker *ben* can also precede this aspectual construction.)

As expected due to the larger number of domains that creoles are used in and the higher input frequency with which their speakers are exposed to constructions, the constructional networks of grammatical constructions of creole languages become more complicated than the ones exhibited by pidgin languages. At the same time, we again find a strong preference for analytic meso-constructions in which each element is assigned a single meaning only (in contrast to the many synthetic tense and aspect constructions of British English).

In exploitation and settlement colonies, it is the third phase of the Dynamic Model, Nativization, that is characterized by greater changes to the constructional networks of the STL and IDG strands. Due to socio-political and historical events (in particular political independence and the resulting identity re-writings), the contact between STL and IDG strand increases significantly. A considerable number of IDG speakers are bilingual at this stage and the innovations of their varieties of English also start to spread to the STL strand (due to the increased contact). Concerning the innovation of structural features, this is a crucial period for these PCEs. As Schneider points out, the new and characteristic structural properties of these varieties seldom involve the creation of patterns that are completely new. Instead, 'at the interface between lexis and grammar' (Schneider 2007: 83), these varieties introduce new syntagmatic combinations and associations of words: thus, Singapore English has *resemble to s.o.* instead of *resemble s.o.* or East African English has *pick s.o.* instead of *pick s.o. up* (cf. also Singapore English and Fiji English) and New Zealand English has *protest sth* instead of *protest against sth* (Schneider 2007: 46–7).

From a Construction Grammar point of view, the structural innovations that surface during Nativization are therefore not completely abstract and schematic macro-constructions. Instead, it is at the meso-constructional level (cf. East African English (SBJ *pick* OBJ) or New Zealand English (SBJ *protest* OBJ)) that idiosyncratic innovations emerge. From a usage-based Construction Grammar perspective, this is actually expected since changes to macro-constructions can normally only occur if they are preceded by significant changes at the subordinate meso-construction level (see Section 2.1). Additionally, first language acquisition data also show that children's first creative uses of language rely on meso-constructions (such as *NOUN get-it*; Diessel 2013; Tomasello 1992) which comprise a constant, substantive element (*get-it*) as well as a schematic slot (here *NOUN*) to produce tokens they might not have heard or said before (such as *Block get-it, Bottle get-it, Phone get-it*, or *Towel get-it*). Only during later stages do children then develop more schematic macro-constructional representations (such NP V).

The first structural innovations of PCEs during the Nativization phase thus seem to follow a pattern that is also observable during first language acquisition: innovations start at the meso-constructional level. Note that this does not mean that PCEs will stop at this stage: as van Rooy (2010: 15) rightly points out, adult learners (here of the IDG group) will be 'able to generalise rules on the basis of less evidence, because their cognitive abilities to notice patterns are more advanced'. Thus, due to their advanced cognitive skills, L2 learners might be able to generalise faster from meso-constructions to more abstract macro-constructions (perhaps even 'too fast' in that they tend to overgeneralize schemas by ignoring exceptions of the L1 system, leading to more regular systems; cf. Szmrecsanyi and Kortmann 2009; van Rooy 2010: 14; for a state-of-the-art summary of Construction Grammar research on L2 acquisition, cf. Ellis 2013). Note, however, that Ellis and Ferreira-Junior (2009) have shown that L2 learners still seem to rely more on prototypical meso-constructions than L1 speakers. Besides, even if L2 learners might arrive more quickly at taxonomic constructional networks with macro-constructions, it does not follow that they do not generalize to a meso-constructional level first. From a usage-based Construction Grammar perspective, it is therefore not surprising that the **first** structural innovations of PCEs occur at the interface between lexis and grammar (see above), that is, at the meso-constructional level even if, in a next step, more abstract macro-constructions might be added more quickly to the construction of L2 learners (than would be expected for L1 learners) – but see below for a further discussion of this issue.

The next phase of the Dynamic Model, Endonormative Stabilization, sees a stabilization of the newly created taxonomic constructional networks. After independence, members of the STL and the IDG strand rewrite their (sociolinguistic) identities and construct themselves as citizens of their newly founded countries. As a consequence, the PCE variety is perceived as fairly stable and homogeneous (Schneider 2007: 51; Buschfeld et al. 2014).

In contrast to this, the final phase, Differentiation, is characterized by 'dialect birth', the rise of regional and social varieties (Schneider 2007: 53–4). Once the new nations have established themselves, the stable citizen identities allow speakers to create new group memberships along other sociolinguistic categories (such as gender, class, region, etc.; Buschfeld et al. 2014). From a Construction Grammar point of view, these processes of dialect birth in PCEs involve the functional realignment and innovation of constructions as linguistic means of identity (Le Page and Tabouret-Keller 1985). Since limitations of space do not allow for an in-depth discussion of these issues, I refer the reader to Hollmann (2013) for an overview of the potential contribution of Construction Grammar to (cognitive) sociolinguistics.

As shown above, the CxG-DM adds a cognitive explanation to the sociolinguistic Dynamic Model. In addition, it makes predictions concerning the qualitative type and quantitative distribution of innovative constructions in post-colonial Englishes (Hoffmann 2014, 2019, 2020): structural innovations of post-colonial Englishes are expected to surface first during Phase III (Nativization) and to appear 'at the interface between lexis and grammar' (Schneider 2007: 83, such as new prepositional verbs or new complementation patterns). From a Construction Grammar point of view, these first new structures will not be fully schematic patterns, but will be partly substantive, partly schematic meso-constructional templates. In addition to these qualitative innovations, in line with constructionist L2 research (Ellis 2013; Ellis and Ferreira-Junior 2009) we can also expect quantitative effects: in earlier phases of the Dynamic Model, post-colonial Englishes will be used in fewer domains and speakers will, therefore, receive less input for a construction. As a result of this lower type frequency, varieties at earlier phases of the Dynamic Model can be expected to rely more on meso-constructions (such as the REFUSE.Verb-Specific construction; cf. Figure 1 and the discussion of macro- and meso-constructions in Section 2.1) and to exhibit a lower productivity of constructional slots. Hoffmann (2014, 2019) illustrated this for the Comparative Correlative construction (*the* (comparative phrase) (clause), *the* (comparative phrase) (clause), e.g., *the more you eat the fatter you'll get*). He found that Phase III varieties such as Philippine English rely more on several specific comparative word combinations such as *higher . . . lower* or *more . . . more* (Hoffmann 2014: 175). In contrast, more advanced varieties such as Jamaican English (Phase IV) only exhibited one significant comparative phrase combination (*more . . . greater*), and the variability of comparative phrases in the native variety British English was so high that no single combination of words is statistically significant (Hoffmann 2014: 175–6). In a similar vein, Bruckmaier (2017: 84) showed that speakers of New Englishes 'cling . . . to and overuse . . . simple and familiar patterns' in the complementation of GET, by preferring monotransitive uses with the standard meaning 'obtain' and under-using rarer patterns such as the ditransitive complementation of GET. Finally, Hoffmann (2011: 270) identified a preference for 'prototypical realizations' among different forms of preposition stranding and pied piping in Kenyan English (a Phase III variety). All of these findings seem to imply that the number of schematic slots in constructions, as well as their productivity, tend to correlate with a variety's stage in Schneider's model: concerning the creative use of constructions, more advanced varieties are expected to exhibit greater slot prod-uctivity and should, correspondingly, rely less on specific, substantive fillers. Recently, a handful of studies have emerged that seem to support this hypothesis (Brunner and Hoffmann 2020; Hoffmann 2020; Laporte 2019). In this Element, I present three studies that test this Dynamic Model Productivity hypothesis.

Dynamic Model Productivity hypothesis: Varieties in later phases of the Dynamic Model show (1) more productivity of the slots of (semi-)schematic construction than varieties in earlier developmental phases due to (2) less reliance on prototypical and frequent fillers.

Note that the Dynamic Model Productivity hypothesis assumes that all varieties are subject to the same cognitive constraints, but that as the input frequency of constructions (and their domains of use) increases, so the

World Englishes

underlying constructional templates become more and more abstract and schematic. As a result, we expect Phase V varieties to exhibit the greatest productivity of slots, and consequently to have entrenched the most abstract meso- and macro-constructions. At the same time, this hypothesis does not imply that all varieties of the same phase have entrenched exactly the same kind of meso- or macro-constructions. Mukherjee and Gries (2009) tested the interaction of verbs and three types of constructional patterns (ditransitive, transitive and intransitive uses) in three Asian varieties (Phase III: Hong Kong, Phase III–IV: Indian and Phase IV: Singapore English) against British English data. They found that the phase of the varieties correlated positively with the number of innovative uses: the more advanced a variety was in the Dynamic Model, the more different its uses of verbs in the various complementation patterns from British English. As varieties evolve along the Dynamic Model stages, they will thus become more and more unlike British English (and, potentially each other) with respect to the precise lexical fillers they employ. At the same time, however, cognitive processes will ensure that varieties at the same stage will be similar with respect to the productivity of their constructional templates (Laporte 2019).

3 Data and Methodology

3.1 Corpus Data and the CxG-DM

As discussed in Section 2.1, usage-based constructionist approaches assume that, in addition to domain-general cognitive processes (such as, e.g., categorization and chunking, as well as schematization), the entrenchment of constructions to a large extent depends on the (type and token) input frequency with which a speaker hears and/or uses it. Fundamentally, entrenchment is a property of the mental grammar of an individual (Blumenthal-Dramé 2012, 2017; Schmid 2020; Stefanowitsch and Flach 2017: 101). This raises the question as to which linguistic data sources can be used to assess the degree of entrenchment of a construction. Bybee, for instance, argues for a wide range of data sources to be adduced:

> In usage-based theory, where grammar is directly based on linguistic experience, there are no types of data that are excluded from consideration because they are considered to represent performance rather than competence. Evidence from child language, psycholinguistic experiments, speakers' intuitions, distribution in corpora and language change are all considered viable sources of evidence about cognitive representations, provided we understand the different factors operating in each of the settings that give rise to the data. (Bybee 2010: 10)

Out of all the data types Bybee mentions, corpora are probably the most widely used data source in current usage-based Construction Grammar (for an overview, see Gries 2013: 97–101). Modern corpora are carefully collected finite-sized samples that strive to be 'maximally representative of the language variety under consideration' (McEnery and Wilson 1996: 24). Methodologically, corpus data have the advantage of being authentic, natural, observational data (Gries 2013: 94–6) that can be considered objective as well as valid and reliable data sources of linguistic usage (Hoffmann 2011: 10). Like all data sources, however, corpus data also have their limitations (Hoffmann 2011: 9–14):

(1) There is the 'positive data problem': just because an utterance occurs in a corpus does not automatically mean that it is grammatical (since it can also be a performance phenomenon; e.g., a false start or self-repair structure).

(2) In addition to this, there is the 'negative data problem': the absence of a structure from a corpus does not entail its ungrammaticality (since it might be missing due to mere chance or register effects).

Nevertheless, the great advantage of corpus data is obviously that they provide natural, authentic data that can be analysed for frequency and context effects.

Still, while corpora thus constitute an important data source for the investigation of language use of a speech community, the question remains whether they allow us any insight into the degree of entrenchment of an individual. Some, like Blumenthal-Dramé (2012, 2017), for example, argue that, as aggregate data from several different speakers, corpus data alone are not suitable for the study of entrenchment (see also Schmid 2020). As Stefanowitsch and Flach (2017: 122) concede, corpus data are not 'typically representative of the input, let alone the output of a particular individual'. Nevertheless, following Schmid's 'from-corpus-to-cognition principle', they point out that text frequency 'instantiates entrenchment in the cognitive system' (2000: 39) in two complementary ways. First of all, there is the 'corpus-as-output' view that argues that, taking into account the effects of domain-general principles, authentic corpus data can be used to draw 'inferences about the mental representations underlying this behavior' (Stefanowitsch and Flach 2017: 102–3). Secondly, the 'corpus-as-input' view advocates that corpus data can be taken as a representative sample of the input that speakers of a speech community are exposed to and which consequently shape their mental construction networks (Stefanowitsch and Flach 2017: 103).

Corpus data can thus be said to offer one, but obviously not the only, window onto the entrenchment of constructions. Psycholinguistic experiments, without doubt, offer a more direct access to the entrenchment of structures in the individual, but also have disadvantages (due to their unnatural setting and the unnatural types of stimuli and responses that are often used; see Gries 2013: 94–5). In light of this, several studies have argued for complementary data sources to be used as converging or corroborating evidence and these have, indeed, shown that the results from experimental and corpus-based studies often converge (Gries, Hampe and Schönefeld 2005, 2010; Hoffmann 2011; Stefanowitsch and Flach 2017: 121; Wiechmann 2008). Besides, corpora are a reliable source for the statistical analysis of positive data with respect to frequency and context phenomena. This is particularly true if they constitute 'big data' (i.e., have a size larger than one billion words). For our purposes, such large corpora allow us to investigate the CxG-DM productivity hypothesis even for constructions that are only mildly frequent (and which consequently hardly appear in older one-million-word corpora).

3.2 The GloWbE Corpus

All data for this Element come from the POS-tagged corpus of Web-based Global English (GloWbE: www.english-corpora.org/glowbe/), which comprises 1.9 billion words from twenty national varieties of English (including British English). Around 60 per cent of the data are scraped from internet blogs (B), while about 40 per cent are taken from 'general websites' (G). Currently, there are still important questions that require answers concerning the reliability and validity of the corpus (e.g., are data automatically scraped from the web fully representative of the sampled varieties?). Consequently, any results from GloWbE will have to be taken with a grain of salt and checked against other data sources (including sociolinguistic interview data or psycholinguistic experiments). At the same time, at present, it is by far the largest corpus of postcolonial Englishes available, and, due to its sheer size, the only potential source for the study of constructions that have such a low token frequency that they cannot be searched in more carefully sampled corpora such as the ones from the International Corpus of English project (ICE)[2] (cf. Nelson, Wallis and Aarts 2002), which only comprise one million words each.

Largely based on Schneider's seminal work (2007), Brunner and Hoffmann (2020; see also Hoffmann 2020) classified the varieties in the GloWbE corpus according to Dynamic Model phase as shown in Table 1.

Note that the above classification from Schneider (2007) is widely accepted and can be argued to constitute a reasonably solid ground for the present Element. At the same time, it is not uncontroversial, as several studies have

---

[2] www.ice-corpora.uzh.ch/en.html.

Table 1 Classification of varieties investigated according to Dynamic Model phase

Phase I	Phase II	Phase III	Phase IV	Phase V
Foundation	Exonormative Stabilization	Nativization	Endonormative Stabilization	Differentiation
–	Bangladeshi English Pakistani English	Philippine English Malaysian English Indian English Kenyan English Tanzanian English Nigerian English Hong Kong English Sri Lanka English Ghana English	Singaporean English Jamaican English	American English Australian English New Zealand English Canadian English Irish English South African English

argued that particular varieties should be assigned to different phases. Mukherjee (2007) suggests that Indian English is in Phase 4; similarly, Borlongan (2016) argues that Philippine English has approached Phase 4 (but see Martin 2014 for a critical discussion of this claim). For South African English, van Rooy (2014) contends that it is in Phase 4, while Mesthrie (2014: 59) claims that 'the varieties of English in present-day South Africa fall into Stage 5'. It is important to remember that any broad classification of post-colonial Englishes is merely an abstraction that glosses over many important differences between the various varieties as well as any intra-variety variation. Schneider (2007), therefore, repeatedly emphasizes that the phases above should only be seen as convenient shortcuts for the complex developmental processes that each variety has undergone (and/or is currently undergoing). Besides, as mentioned in Section 3.1, corpus data can only be considered a proxy for psycholinguistic data. Nevertheless, I maintain that a big data source such as the GloWbE corpus enables researchers to put hypotheses such as the Dynamic Model Productivity hypothesis to a first test. Future studies will then need to draw on other empirical sources (such as sociolinguistic interviews; Bhatt and Mesthrie 2008: 42–43; or psycholinguistic experiments) to test whether the Dynamic Model Productivity hypothesis also is supported by these data from individual speakers of the various post-colonial Englishes.

Next, I would like to address another methodological issue: while the GloWbE corpus is, currently, one of the largest of the corpora of World Englishes, any statistical analysis of data from it will have to take into account that its subcorpora differ considerably in size.

As Figure 3 shows, the size of data sampled for the various varieties in GloWbE ranges from 387,615,074 words (GB) to 35,169,042 words (Tanzania) (see www.english-corpora.org/glowbe/). A comparison of raw frequencies of any phenomenon across varieties will, therefore, give misleading results (simply because the corpus contains ten times as much data for British English than for Tanzanian English). Instead, statistical tests have to be used that take into account these differences in sample size.

3.3 Variables and Statistical Tests

A major claim of the Dynamic Model Productivity hypothesis (Section 2.3) is the claim that varieties in earlier stages of the Dynamic Model exhibit less productivity of the slots of (semi-)schematic construction than varieties in later developmental stages. In order to test the productivity of slots, I submitted all data to a 'Large Number of Rare Events' (LNRE) model (Baroni and Evert 2014; Zeldes 2013). Slot productivity has received considerable attention in

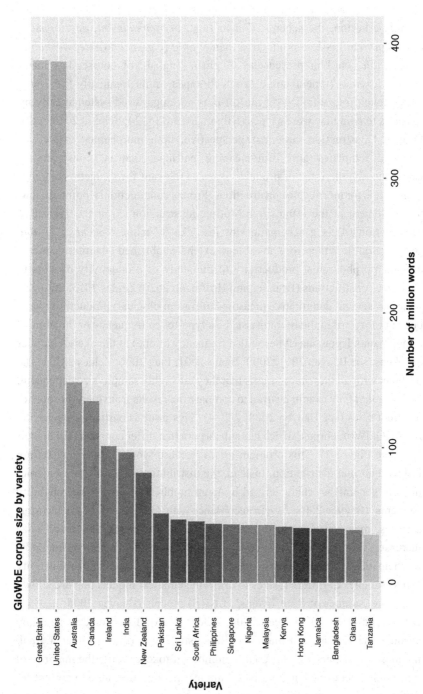

Figure 3 Size of variety-based subcorpora in **GloWbE**

morphological studies, where it is regularly conceptualized as the ability of a morpheme to license new types (see Plag 2003: 44–51; Schmid 2016: 111–16). By this criterion, the schema V-*ment* (e.g., *accompaniment*, *development*, *settlement*, etc.) is less productive than V-*able* (e.g., *achievable*, *washable*, *translatable*, etc.) in present-day English. English, of course, has many V-*ment* lexemes (types), some of which appear quite frequently (i.e., have a high token frequency) – yet the suffix is no longer used systematically by speakers to coin new words/types (Hilpert 2013: 115–24; Schmid 2016: 112). From a Construction Grammar perspective, both morphemes as well as syntactic templates are form–meaning pairings, that is, constructions. Consequently, the issue of productivity is as relevant for syntactic constructions as it is for morpheme constructions. From a constructionist point of view, the V element in the Intransitive Motion construction (3) or the Transitive construction (4) is a schematic slot just like V in the V-*ment* or V-*able* construction. It is therefore possible to extend established quantitative measures of morphological productivity to the study of productivity of slots in syntactic constructions (Brunner and Hoffmann 2020; Zeldes 2013: 266–72).

So far, several quantitative measures of (morphological) productivity have been put forward in the literature such as type-token frequency or the proportion of hapax legomena (types with a frequency of one) in the overall number of tokens (see Baayen 2001, 2009; Bauer 2001; Plag 2006; Zeldes 2013). The problem with all these measures is that they are highly sample-size dependent, meaning that they cannot be used to compare the results from (sub-)corpora of different sizes (see Baayen 2008: 222–4). This issue is particularly pressing for the GloWbE corpus, which has subcorpora that differ considerably in their size (see Figure 3). This problem arises because words in any text do not follow a normal distribution. Instead, the distribution of words (or constructions in general) is 'characterized by large numbers of very low probability elements' (Baayen 2008: 229; in accordance with Zipf's Law). In small corpus samples, many new types can be found at first. Yet, as the sample size increases, the likelihood of encountering new types decreases considerably. Mathematically, it is thus necessary for the measure of linguistic productivity across samples of different sizes to draw on statistical models that are known as 'Large Number of Rare Events' (LNRE) models (Baayen 2008: 229–36; Baroni and Evert 2014; Evert 2004; Zeldes 2013). These models take into account the Zipfian distribution of linguistic items (the fact that a small number of types account for a large number of tokens, while the majority of types only occur once in any given sample) and are, thus, able to correct for differences in sample size when measuring productivity across samples from corpora of varying size. For this reason, we used Evert and Baroni's (2007) zipfR[3] package to measure and plot the productivity of constructional slots to test the Dynamic Model Productivity hypothesis. Using finite Zipf-Mandelbrot models (Evert 2004), the package makes it possible to fit LNRE models to frequency data by random sampling and extrapolating vocabulary growth curves from the data. In simpler terms, the package tracks the number of new types as the sample size increases (its 'vocabulary growth'). It then does not project the productivity of a pattern in a linear fashion (since new types become rarer and rarer as sample size increases). Instead, LNRE models project the productivity of a schematic slot beyond the empirical sample size by predicting a curve that first rises steeply and then seems to flatten (since it is a type of cumulative distribution function of an exponential type of distribution). For details on the mathematical background of LNRE models, see Baayen (2008: 229–36) and Baroni and Evert (2014).

A second prediction of the Dynamic Model Productivity hypothesis is that varieties at earlier stages of the Dynamic Model show a greater reliance on fewer and more prototypical and frequent fillers than varieties at later stages. While LNRE models already test the overall productivity of patterns, they obviously can not identify particular prototypical patterns that might be employed by a variety. After all, it is a purely quantitative method that merely identifies the rate at which new types are discovered in a sample. Finding potential prototypical constructional fillers requires the investigation of associations between categorical variables (such as a filler slot and a Dynamic Model phase). Therefore, to test for such effects, we assess the statistical preference of certain fillers in constructional slots by Dynamic Model phase using Configural Frequency Analyses (CFAs). CFAs identify any combination of two or more factors that is significantly more frequent (so-called 'types') or infrequent (so-called 'antitypes'; Gries 2009: 244) than expected by chance. CFAs test the deviation of each individual cell for significance and thus allow for a finely grained assessment of statistical correlations (e.g., if a verbal filler co-occurs significantly more frequently with varieties in Phase V). All *p*-values are automatically corrected for multiple testing, and exact, non-parametric tests are used whenever token numbers are too low for chi-square tests (Gries 2004). An important caveat of CFAs, however, is that they are fairly conservative and that for many phenomena, despite the overall size of the GloWbE corpus, the token numbers from Phase II and Phase IV varieties will be too low to detect significant effects (Brunner and Hoffmann 2020). Nevertheless, in all cases, the CFAs should allow meaningful comparisons of the British (GB) variety versus

---

[3] Available at: http://zipfR.R-Forge.R-Project.org/.

Phase III and Phase V varieties (since the GloWbE corpus contains sufficiently large samples for these variety types).

4 Sample Studies

Next, I present three studies that explicitly test the Dynamic Model Productivity hypothesis.

4.1 *Way* Construction

Brunner and Hoffmann (2020) investigated the *Way* construction, examples of which are given in (13):

(13)   a. **the boy works his way into the lives of a middle class family** (GloWbE-GB-B)

   b. **You also insinuate your way into the media** (GloWbE-GB-B)

   c. politicians going around in ceremahs speaking of war against corruption when **they are smiling their way to the bank** at the same time (GloWbE-MY-G)

   (data from Brunner and Hoffmann 2020).

The *Way* construction is part of the so-called family of argument structure constructions – abstract, schematic constructions that are considered to encode basic human event construals (Goldberg 1995: 224–5; Langacker 1991): the *Way* construction, for example, expresses a scene in which a subject (*the boy* (13a), *you* (13b), *they* (13c)) moves along a path designated by the prepositional phrase (*into the lives of a middle class family* (13a), *into the media* (13b), *to the bank* (13c)). It is thus a construal that is semantically related with Intransitive Motion construction (3). What makes the *Way* construction idiomatic is that it can host non-movement predicates in its verb slot (*work* (13a), *insinuate* (13b), *smile* (13c)) and that it has an obligatory NP headed by the noun *way*, which is preceded by a possessive pronoun that must be co-referential with the subject (*the boy* → *his way* (13a), *you* → *your way* (13b), *they* → *their way* (13c)). Example (14) provides the constructional template that underlies all these uses:

(14)   *Way* construction
    FORM: SBJ_1 V_2 [$POSS_1$ *way*] OBL_{PP3}
    $\leftrightarrow$
    MEANING: 'PARTICIPANT$_1$ traverse the PATH$_{PP3}$ while/by doing V_2'
    (adapted from Traugott and Trousdale 2013: 79).

The template consists of a subject SBJ_1 (normally realized by an NP) followed by a verb V_2, the noun *way* with a possessive determiner $POSS_1$ (which must be co-referential with the subject, hence the identical subscript number '1'), and an adverbial prepositional phrase OBL. In its most prototypical instantiation, it expresses the idea that the subject NP moves along a path designated by the prepositional phrase (for further details cf. Brunner and Hoffmann 2020). Now, nominal slots such as SBJ and the NP complement of the PP in the OBL position can be expected to show high productivity across all varieties, since they are referential constructions that appear widely across a great number of argument structure constructions (Goldberg 2019: 59–60). In contrast, the relationship between verbs and argument structure constructions is much more constrained (Goldberg 2019: 57–8), which is why the following section focuses on the productivity of the V slot of the *Way* construction.

All in all, Brunner and Hoffmann (2020) retrieved 14,771 tokens of the *Way* construction from GloWbE. Table 2 shows how these were distributed across the various Dynamic Model phases (and including British English as a reference point).

The GloWbE corpus contains considerably fewer texts for Phase II and Phase IV varieties, so it is no surprise that these varieties also yield fewer tokens of the *Way* constructions. But what about the productivity of the verb slot? How many different types of the construction do the various phases exhibit? In order to test this, Brunner and Hoffmann (2020) subjected the verb slot data to an LNRE analysis, the results of which can be found in Figure 4. The five curves give the predicted productivity of the construction for each Dynamic Model phase (with the short vertical lines extending from the curves indicating the confidence interval of the models' predictions). In addition, the single, long vertical lines in the figure indicate the empirical token size found in GloWbE, beyond which the lines of the LNRE model are, consequently, model estimates (for Phase II this line is at token size 481, for Phase IV at 684, and so on).

Figure 4 shows the LNRE models for the productivity of the V slot of the *Way* construction in the five Dynamic Model phases. As the figure shows, the LNRE analysis largely supports the Dynamic Model Productivity hypothesis: at the bottom, we find Phase II varieties, which plateau at around 200 different V types once the 2,000 token mark is reached. Patterning with the reference variety British English (GB), Phase V varieties, on the other

Table 2 Tokens of the *Way* construction in GloWbE by Dynamic Model phase

DM phase	II	III	IV	V	GB	Sum
Tokens	481	2,949	684	7,051	3,606	14,771

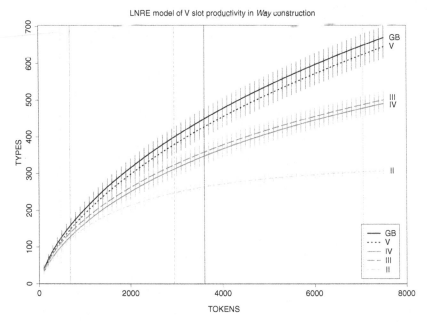

Figure 4 LNRE productivity of the V slot across Dynamic Model phases
(Source: Fig. 1. Way.png under a CC-BY4.0 license at https://osf.io/29b48/)

hand, show the highest productivity of the V slot (with more than 600 different V types). Finally, Phase III and Phase IV varieties pattern together very closely (having overlapping confidence lines) and cover the middle ground.

So far, we have established that the overall productivity of the V slot correlates positively with a variety's Dynamic Model phase. But what about the specific lexical fillers that are used in the *Way* construction across the Dynamic Model phases? Can we also find evidence that varieties at earlier stages rely more on particular prototypical fillers than varieties at later stages? As mentioned above, CFA tests can be used to identify significant associations of categorical variables across phases. For the analyses of the results of CFAs, it has to be remembered that the low sample sizes for Phase II and Phase IV in the GloWbE mean that many effects for these stages will not emerge as significant. For, while CFAs can correct for the unequal size of tokens due to differences in sample size, unlike LNRE models they cannot project effect sizes beyond the actual sample size. Since p-values crucially correlate with sample size, this means that the results for Phase II and Phase IV are going to be conservative (prone to a type II error, i.e., being unable to identify potentially significant effects due to a small sample size).

For the V slot of the *Way* construction, Brunner and Hoffmann (2020: 16–18) find at least partial support for the prototypicality hypothesis: Phase III has two significant V lemmas (*find* (15) and *sleep* (16)), while Phase V only has one lemma (*work* (17); Brunner and Hoffmann 2020: 16):[4]

(15)   some of such donations still **find** their way into the country (GloWbE-GH-G)
(16)   I'm willing to **sleep** my way to the top . . . (GloWbE-IN-G)
(17)   . . . and we'll **work** our way through the Workbook . . . (GloWbE-US-G)

As Brunner and Hoffmann (2020: 16) argue, *find* (15) is a highly prototypical verb for the *Way* construction due to its meaning (since it entails movement in space to locate something and thus is highly compatible with the construction's MEANING: 'PARTICIPANT$_1$ traverse the PATH$_{PP3}$ while/by doing V$_2$') and its high frequency in the corpus at large (as well as in the combination with *way*: *But, all is good after friends help her **find** her **way**.* GloWbE-CA-G). Moreover, *find* is used more frequently in Phase II than any other phase, but this effect does not reach statistical significance (due to the overall low token frequency of Phase II; see above). *Sleep* (16), on the other hand, might be somewhat surprising at first, given the verb's prototypically intransitive meaning. As the data show, however, in the construction it is used in its meaning of 'having intercourse with' and twenty-one out of the thirty-three examples of this pattern come from one variety (Indian English: *I'm willing to **sleep** my way to the top* . . . (GloWbE-IN-G). Finally, *work* (17), which expresses 'movement in the face of difficulty' is not only favoured by Phase V, but also significantly dispreferred by Phase III.

For the *Way* construction, the CFA analysis, therefore, yields some evidence for a quantitative difference with respect to the number of prototypical verb fillers (though the differences are only slight). The semantics of the preferred filler, arguably, shows a stronger prototype effect: while a verb that highlights the endpoint of movement (*find*) is preferred by Phase III varieties, Phase V varieties favour a verb that focuses more on the difficulty of the motion event (*work*). Phase III varieties thus prefer a prototypical construal of the *Way* construction that encodes completed motion (to a goal), while Phase V varieties zoom in more on the (difficult) process of motion (thus enriching the construction's MEANING: 'PARTICIPANT$_1$ traverse the PATH$_{PP}$ **despite difficulties** while/by doing V' in these instances). This conclusion receives further support

---

[4] Brunner and Hoffmann (2020) also identify *pay* as significantly associated with British English. Yet, as they argue, the vast majority of these cases (i.e., fifty out of fifty-five) are instances of the proverbial expression *pay (our|their|its| . . .) way in the world* (cf. *so that Britain can begin to **pay** its way in the world again.* (GloWbE-GB)), which fail to qualify as prototypical instances of the *Way* construction as they lack directional meaning.

when taking into account the prepositional slot: while Phase III varieties favour *to* (which entails completed motion), Phase V varieties favour *through* (which focuses on the concept of difficult motion through an obstacle: *We've just got to* ***fight*** *our way* ***through*** *the situations now and see how the opposition do* (GloWbE-AU-G) or ***Pushing*** *their way* ***through*** *the fire the Romans made their way into* ... (GloWbE-CA-G); Brunner and Hoffmann 2020: 19). Table 3 summarizes the significant V-P associations for GB and Phases V and III.

Table 3 shows that a quantitative difference between the variety types does exist, but that it is very small: Phase III varieties have eleven significant patterns, while GB has twelve and Phase V varieties contain fifteen significant V-P combinations. More important than these numerical differences, however, are the qualitative differences between the variety types. In Phase III, nine of the eleven patterns involve the prepositions *in* and *into*, which signal the goal of a completed motion event. In contrast, GB and Phase V display more variation in the P slot and also contain patterns with the preposition *through* (*work through*, *push through*, *navigate through*) that focus more on the extended meaning of the *Way* construction that can be captured as 'PARTICIPANT$_1$ traverse the PATH$_{PP}$ **despite difficulties** while/by doing V').

Table 3 Significant V-P associations across Dynamic Model phases (verbs ordered according to frequency of occurrence in sample of *Way* constructions; data from Brunner and Hoffmann 2020: 23)

GB	V	III
make to	*make to*	*make to*
find into	*find into*	*find into*
find onto	*work through*	*find to*
work through	*work up*	*work up*
work up	*force into*	*force into*
force into	*push through*	*know around*
navigate through	*navigate through*	*lose in*
know around	*know around*	*come in*
lose in	*lose in*	*sleep to*
pay in	*pay in*	*laugh to*
get in	*come in*	*warm into*
earn in	*get in*	
	learn around	
	commit unto	
	weasel into	

Both the LNRE and the CFA analysis of the *Way* construction provide evidence for the Dynamic Model Productivity hypothesis. Varieties at earlier stages of the Dynamic Model show less productivity of the V slot and have a greater reliance on more prototypical fillers of the V and P slots than varieties in later developmental stages.

4.2 V *the Hell Out of* Construction

Another, albeit much more infrequent, argument structure construction is the V *the hell out of* NP construction (Haïk 2012; Hoeksema and Napoli 2008; Hoffmann 2020; Perek 2016):

(18) Quentin **acts the hell out of** this next scene, ... (GloWbE-US-B)

The V *the hell out of* NP construction is a two-argument construction (*Quentin* and *this next scene* in (18)) that 'generally conveys an intensifying function' (Perek 2016: 165) and normally has a two-participant verb in its V slot. Semantically, the construction incorporates the meaning of the transitive construction (4), with an initiator/agent (*Quentin* in (18)) exercising force onto an endpoint/patient (*this next scene* in (18)). In addition, the idiomatic subpart *the hell out of* adds the intensifying meaning with the taboo word slot being filled by various appropriate items:

(19) a. I thought the villain was incredibly lame. No disrespect to Javier Bardem, that guy could **act the crap out of** any role, but he got a really annoying character to play. (GloWbE-US-B)

b. Michael Fassbender really **acted the shit out of** this one. (GloWbE-AU-G)

As the constructed examples in (20) illustrate, the taboo word, which expresses the intensifying meaning, is an integral part of this construction that cannot be omitted:

(20) a. ... *that guy could **act out of** any role, ...

b. ... *Michael Fassbender really **acted out of** this one.

The constructional template for this marginal argument structure construction can, thus, be represented as follows (21):

(21) V *the* $N_{\text{taboo-word}}$ *out of* construction:
FORM: [SBJ$_1$ V$_2$ [*the* N_{TABOO} *out of*]$_3$ OBJ$_4$]
$\leftrightarrow$
MEANING: ['Instigator/Agent$_1$ doing V$_2$ excessively$_3$ to Endpoint/Patient$_4$']
(adapted from Hoeksema and Napoli 2008; Perek 2016)

Following the procedure of Brunner and Hoffmann (2020), Hoffmann (2020) queried the GloWbE corpus for verbs followed by the *hell/crap/shit/fuck* out, which resulted in 5,627 relevant tokens.[5] Table 4 gives an overview of how these were distributed across British English (GB) as well as Dynamic Model phases subcorpora.

As with the *Way* construction, Figure 5 then provides the results from the LNRE analysis of the type productivity of the V slot of this construction across Dynamic Model phases.

Figure 5 is not completely identical with Figure 4, which is to be expected for variable data. Constructions will have a variable frequency across phases, being used more prominently in some varieties but not in others. Nevertheless, the Dynamic Model Productivity hypothesis is again strongly supported: Phase II varieties exhibit the lowest type productivity, while Phase V varieties show the highest slot productivity curve. Phase III varieties are again higher than Phase II, but considerably lower than Phase IV (which have a productivity curve similar to that of the reference variety British English).

The data for the V *the* $N_{taboo-word}$ *out of* construction thus confirm the quantitative aspect of the Dynamic Model Productivity hypothesis, but what about the prototypicality aspect of the fillers? Let us first look at the choice of taboo noun.

As Figure 6 shows, with respect to the N_{taboo}, the GloWbE data roughly confirm the prototypicality hypothesis: in all variety types, *hell* is the most frequently used taboo N, but at the same time the frequency of *shit* and *fuck* increases. A closer inspection of the GloWbE corpus reveals, however, that this is more of an effect of the overall distribution of these taboo words across the varieties. Table 5 provides the CFA for these selected taboo Ns across the entire GloWbE corpus (including the V *the* $N_{taboo-word}$ *out of* construction).

Table 4 Tokens of the V *the* $N_{taboo-word}$ *out of* construction in GloWbE by Dynamic Model phase

DM phase	II	III	IV	V	GB	Sum
Tokens	79	514	194	3,814	1,026	5,627

---

[5] Note that the token size of Hoffmann (2020) is actually slightly lower (5,506) since it did not include the data for South African English, which is included here (since the other two sample studies presented in this paper also include it).

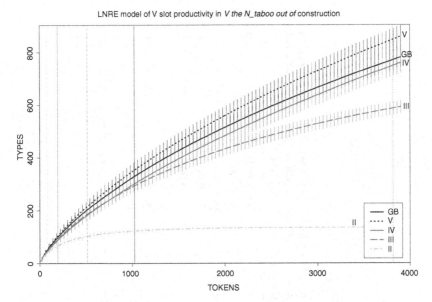

Figure 5 LNRE productivity of the V slot across Dynamic Model phases
(Source: Fig. 2. V-the-hell.png under a CC-BY4.0 license at https://osf.io/svmfy/)

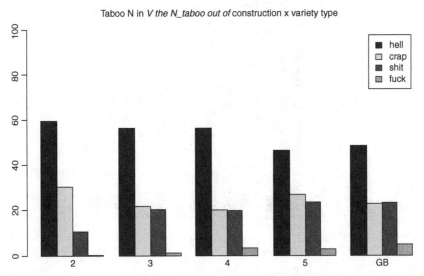

Figure 6 Taboo N in V *the* N_taboo-word *out of* construction across
Dynamic Model phases

The CFA implies that, independently of the V *the* N_taboo-word *out of* construction, the taboo N constructions generally increase in use across the Dynamic Model phases (as predicted by the Dynamic Model

Table 5 CFA of taboo Ns in the whole GloWbE across Dynamic Model phases (n.b. only significant positive associations are provided)

N_{taboo}	STAGE	Freq	Exp	Cont.chisq	Obs-exp	P.adj.Holm	Dec	Q
fuck	GB	6,080	5,216.07	143.09	>	$p < 0.001$	***	0.004
crap	GB	9,545	9,119.90	19.81	>	$p < 0.001$	***	0.002
fuck	V	14,127	13,865.37	4.94	>	$p < 0.05$	*	0.001
crap	V	26,263	24,242.53	168.39	>	$p < 0.001$	***	0.011
shit	V	31,746	29,972.27	104.97	>	$p < 0.001$	***	0.01
fuck	IV	997	866.74	19.58	>	$p < 0.001$	***	0.001
shit	IV	2,131	1,873.61	35.36	>	$p < 0.001$	***	0.001
hell	III	16,060	11,967.95	1,399.14	>	$p < 0.001$	***	0.021
hell	II	3,705	2,219.37	994.47	>	$p < 0.001$	***	0.007

Table 6 CFA of taboo Ns in V *the* $N_{taboo\text{-}word}$ *out of* construction across Dynamic Model phases (n.b. only significant positive associations are provided)

N_{taboo}	PHASE	Freq	Exp	Cont. chisq	Obs-exp	P.adj. Holm	Dec	Q
fuck	GB	51	29.90	14.88	>	p < 0.01	**	0.0004

Productivity hypothesis): while Phase II and III varieties significantly favour only one taboo N (*hell*), Phase IV has two significant taboo words (*fuck/shit*) and Phase V favour three taboo Ns (*fuck/crap/shit*).[6] Once the overall distribution of taboo words is taken into account, it is not surprising that in the V *the* $N_{taboo\text{-}word}$ *out of* construction only one taboo word and Dynamic Model phase association is identified as significant (*fuck* appears significantly more frequently in the construction in GB) (see Table 6).

In a next step, I tested the V lemma x N_{taboo} filler combinations across Dynamic Model phases.

As Table 7 shows, the sample size is too small to yield significant effects for Phase II and IV. Moreover, the results in this case do not provide clear support for the Dynamic Model Productivity hypothesis: all types of varieties have V + N_{taboo} combinations that include a verb that encodes physical force transfer (GB: KICK *the shit out of* / V: BEAT *the crap out of* / III: BEAT *the crap out of*). This meaning of physical force transfer is, obviously, perfectly prototypical for the construction at hand (MEANING: 'Instigator/Agent$_1$ doing V excessively$_2$ to Endpoint/Patient$_3$'). The only pattern that can be argued to be less prototypical (ENJOY *the hell out of*), since it does not entail physical force, can be found in Phase V.

So far, I relied only on the specific lexical lemmas that were used in a slot to identify prototypical meso-constructions. Since the V *the* N_{taboo} *out of*-dataset is not too large (< 6,000 tokens), it is also possible to annotate its semantics using a more sophisticated constructional method. In usage-based Construction Grammar, the meaning pole of constructions is not taken to be truth-conditional. Instead, mental meaning is believed to be encyclopedic in nature. Thus, the meaning of *apple* is not just 'apple', but includes knowledge about what apples look like, where and when they grow, how they taste, etc. This linguistic approach to meaning is known as frame semantics (cf. Boas and Dux 2017; Fillmore 1977, 1982, 1985, 2006; Fillmore and Baker 2010).

---

[6] Since the overall data size of this sample of taboo words (N = 207,193) is considerably bigger than that of the other studies, it should not be surprising that even Phase II and IV provide more significant CFA effects.

Table 7 CFA of taboo N x V in V *the* $N_{\text{taboo-word}}$ *out of* construction across Dynamic Model phases (n.b. only significant positive associations are provided)

V	N_{TABOO}	PHASE	Freq	Exp	Cont.chisq	Obs-exp	P.adj.Holm	Dec	Q
kick	*shit*	GB	38	10.19	75.91	>	$p < 0.001$	***	0.005
beat	*crap*	V	270	166.51	64.32	>	$p < 0.001$	***	0.019
enjoy	*hell*	V	56	28.51	26.52	>	$p < 0.05$	*	0.005
beat	*crap*	III	54	22.44	44.39	>	$p < 0.001$	***	0.006

The major claim of this approach is that mental knowledge is represented cognitively in so-called semantic frames: knowledge structures that contain information on those participant roles that are highlighted or 'profiled' by a concept (e.g., the sender, recipient and entity that is sent in the sending frame) as well as all semantically presupposed, 'background' information of event types (including, e.g., the fact that sending events involve transfer from a source, a fact that normally is not verbalized in English; cf. Croft 2012: 11). A classic example is the commerce frame, which involves the core frame elements SELLER, BUYER, GOODS and MONEY. Specific lexical items such as BUY, SELL or COST activate the entire commerce frame, but also highlight certain frame elements.

(22)   a. *Bill*$_\text{BUYER}$ *bought a new guitar*$_\text{GOODS}$ (*from Steve*$_\text{SELLER}$) (*for 100\$*$_\text{MONEY}$)

   b. *Steve*$_\text{SELLER}$ *sold Bill*$_\text{BUYER}$ *a new guitar*$_\text{GOODS}$ (*for 100\$*$_\text{MONEY}$)

   c. *This guitar*$_\text{GOODS}$ costs *100\$*$_\text{MONEY}$

As (22) shows, BUY foregrounds the frame roles of BUYER and GOODS (while SELLER and MONEY are optional), while SELL highlights the SELLER, the BUYER and the GOODS and COST focuses on the GOODS and the MONEY.

For the present study, it was possible to draw on a dataset provided by FrameNet (https://framenet.icsi.berkeley.edu/fndrupal/[7]) that contained 10,466 lexical units which are associated with 1,075 frames. Using an R script, the verb lemmas of the V *the* N_taboo *out of* construction were automatically tagged for the semantic frame with which they are associated. Since verbs are often used in several different frames, all frame annotations had to be checked manually. The frames that were most frequently evoked by the V *the* N_taboo *out of* construction turned out to be the following ones (n.b. 'FE' here stands for 'Frame Element'):

• **Attack**: An Assailant physically attacks a Victim (which is usually but not always sentient), causing or intending to cause the Victim physical damage. A Weapon used by the Assailant may also be mentioned, in addition to the usual Place, Time, Purpose, Explanation, etc. Sometimes a location is used metonymically to stand for the Assailant or the Victim, and in such cases the Place FE will be annotated on a second FE layer.[8]
  [example lemmas: *attack, bomb* (only two)
  example of construction: *if there's something I don't like,* ***I will attack the shit out of it*** *on my own sites* (GloWbE-NZ-G)]

- **Cause-harm**: The words in this frame describe situations in which an Agent or a Cause injures a Victim The Body_part of the Victim which is most directly affected may also be mentioned in the place of the Victim. In such cases, the Victim is often indicated as a genitive modifier of the Body_part, in which case the Victim FE is indicated on a second FE layer.[9]

  [example lemmas: *bash, beat, flog, hammer*

  example of construction: ***he beat the hell out of me*** (GloWbE-GH-B)]

- **Cause_to_fragment**: An Agent suddenly and often violently separates the Whole_patient into two or more smaller Pieces, resulting in the Whole_patient no longer existing as such. Several lexical items are marked with the semantic type Negative, which indicates that the fragmentation is necessarily judged as injurious to the original Whole_patient.[10]

  [example lemmas: *break, dissect, rip*

  example of construction: *And while there's not much you can do to what has been written in a magazine you can choose* ***to rip the fuck out it*** *and never buy it again!* (GloWbE-SG-B)]

- **Experiencer_focused_emotion**: The words in this frame describe an Experiencer's emotions with respect to some Content. Although the Content may refer to an actual, current state of affairs, quite often it refers to a general situation which causes the emotion.[11]

  [example lemmas: *dig sth., fear, love, hate, like*

  example of construction: ***She loved the crap out of Addy*** ... (GloWbE-US-B)]

- **Stimulate_emotion:** Some phenomenon (the Stimulus) provokes a particular emotion in an Experiencer.[12]

  [example lemmas: *please, surprise, hate, worry, annoy, like*

  example of construction: *Doesn't have to be much,* ***just enough to surprise the shit out of them***. (GloWbE-IE-G)]

As the above list of frames shows, semantically we can identify two subtypes of V *the* N$_{taboo}$ *out of* construction: one in which the verb expresses physical transfer of force (cf. the frames Attack, Cause_harm and Cause_to_fragment) and another one in which the transfer of force is psychological with an Experiencer being mentally affected by the event denoted by the construction (cf. the frames Experiencer_focused_emotion and Stimulate_emotion). Figure 7 gives an

---

[9] https://framenet2.icsi.berkeley.edu/fnReports/data/frameIndex.xml?frame=Cause_harm.

[10] https://framenet2.icsi.berkeley.edu/fnReports/data/frameIndex.xml?frame=Cause_to_fragment.

[11] https://framenet2.icsi.berkeley.edu/fnReports/data/frameIndex.xml?frame=Experiencer _focused_emotion.

[12] https://framenet2.icsi.berkeley.edu/fnReports/data/frameIndex.xml?frame=Stimulate_emotion.

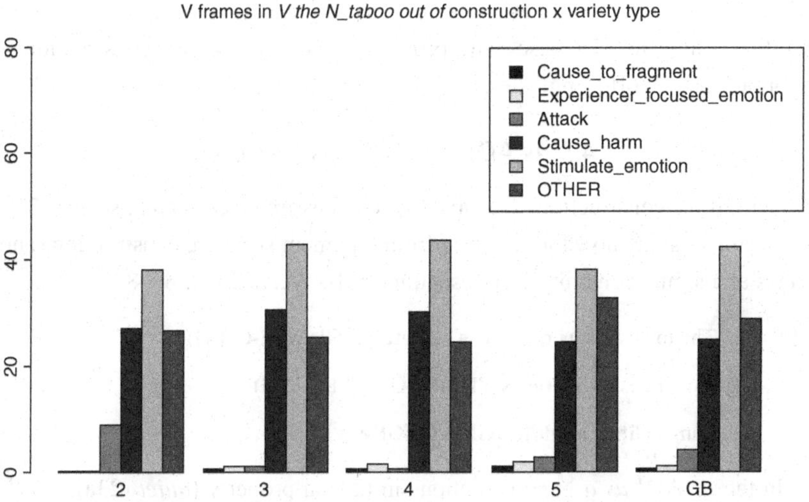

V frames in *V the N_taboo out of* construction x variety type

Figure 7 Semantic frames evoked by V lemma in V *the* N_{taboo} *out of* construction across the various Dynamic Model phases

overview of the distribution of all these frames in the V *the* N_{taboo} *out of* construction across the various Dynamic Model phases.

As can be seen in Figure 7, across all variety types the Simulate_emotion frame is the one that is most frequently evoked by the V lemma (e.g. SURPRISE, HATE or ANNOY), accounting for about 40 per cent of all uses of the construction (e.g., *My husband also likes to scare the crap out out of the kids.* (GloWbE-US-G)). The most frequent frame that encodes (excessive) transfer of physical force, Cause_harm, makes up 25–30 per cent of all cases. All types of varieties thus seem to possess both types of meanings: transfer of physical force and transfer of psychological force. In addition, there are other, minor preferences that can be observed: Phase II has the highest percentage of the Attack frame (accounting for 8.9 per cent of all Phase II tokens). In contrast, Phase V and GB show a larger percentage of frames other than the five mentioned above (OTHER V = 32.4 per cent and OTHER GB = 28.5 per cent), thus, again, implying a greater type frequency. Yet, none of these effects emerges as significant in the CFA test of these configurations.

Nevertheless, even though the frame semantic analysis did not provide strong support of the Dynamic Model Productivity hypothesis, it helped to identify two subconstructions of the V *the* N_{taboo} *out of* construction (one expressing physical transfer of force from an agent to a patient, with the other focusing more on how a stimulus mentally affected an experiencer). Regardless of whether future research will find further support for or might eventually falsify the Dynamic

Model Productivity hypothesis, I believe that frame semantic analyses drawing on the FrameNet database will provide a useful tool for constructionist approaches to World Englishes.

4.3 *As* ADJ *as a* N Construction

So far, all the constructions we have looked at expressed dynamic scenes. The final sample study now moves away from argument structure constructions and looks at a simile construction (Desagulier 2016; Veale 2012: 67–80):

(23)   a. The town was **as quiet as a cemetery**. (GloWbE-GH-G)

b. Now he is **as gentle as a lamb.** (GloWbE-LK-G)

c. I am **as fit as a fiddle**. (GloWbE-GB-G)

In the *as* ADJ *as a* N constructions in (23), a property (*quiet* (23a), *gentle* (23b), *fit* (23c)) that is seen as typical of a noun (*cemetery* (23a), *lamb* (23b), *fiddle* (23c)) is attributed to a referent phrase outside of the construction (in many cases the subject of the clause in which the *as* ADJ *as a* N construction functions as a subject complement; cf. *the town* (23a), *he* (23b), *I* (23c)). Similar to metaphors, such similes link two cognitive domains based on same perceived conceptual similarity (Dancygier 2017: 608–12). As with all constructions, some of the utterances created by it will become entrenched as idioms (23c). In addition to these, however, productive new instances (23b, 23c) also appear which can be captured by the following constructional template:

(24)   *As* ADJ *as a* N construction:
        FORM: [as ADJ$_1$ as a N$_2$]
        ↔
        MEANING: ['X has PROPERTY$_1$ similar to Entity$_2$']

The construction in (24) has two slots (one for the ADJ and one for the N). A query of the GloWbE corpus for this pattern yields 9,671 tokens. As before, Table 8 breaks down the distribution of these across the Dynamic Model phases.

In contrast to the preceding two structures, the simile construction has two slots that are closely related, since ADJ and N correlate with each other (and are taken to be related within a cognitive domain). In light of this, the combined ADJ-N pairs (such as *quiet-cemetery* (23a), *gentle-lamb* (23b) and *fit-fiddle* (23c)) were subjected to a combined LNRE analysis.

As Figure 8 shows, the construction is a highly productive one across all phases. In fact, it is by far the most productive one out of the three sample studies: even Phase II varieties, which show the least productive use by far, are predicted to reach more than 2,000 types once 5,000 tokens are sampled.

Table 8 Tokens of the *as* ADJ *as a* N construction in GloWbE by Dynamic Model phase

DM phase	II	III	IV	V	GB	Sum
Tokens	278	1,819	347	4,867	2,333	9,671

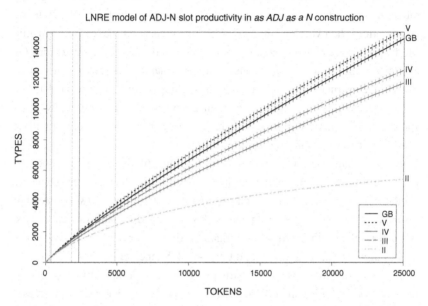

Figure 8 LNRE productivity of the ADJ-N slot across Dynamic Model phases (Source: Fig. 3. as-ASJ-as_N.png under a CC-BY4.0 license at https://osf.io/d58fr/)

Nevertheless, we see a pattern similar to the one exhibited by the other two studies: Phase V varieties show the highest productivity rate (even higher than the British English reference variety), while Phase II varieties have the lowest productivity. Phase IV and Phase III can be found in between these two extremes (with Phase IV, however, significantly superseding Phase III varieties).

The quantitative analysis of the LNRE model thus, once again, supports the Dynamic Model Productivity hypothesis: the Dynamic Model phase of a variety correlates positively with the quantitative productivity of constructional slots. Yet, the productivity of the *as* ADJ *as a* N construction is so high that the GloWbE data exhibit no single, significant ADJ-N pair in the CFA analysis. Gries's (2004) HCFA script does not even converge, and when using the alternative CFA library, we can see why: the 9,671 GloWbE tokens comprise 7,493 unique ADJ-N types. Moreover, only one ADJ-N pair (*as good as a man* in Phase V) has an expected frequency higher than five (5.83). The simile construction is thus an extremely flexible and versatile pattern that is used frequently across all variety types.

5 Conclusion

All three case studies presented in this paper support the constructionist Dynamic Model Productivity hypothesis: varieties at earlier phases of the model are, in general, expected to exhibit a lower productivity of schematic constructions than varieties in later phases. At the same time, earlier Dynamic Model phases are characterized by more prototypical uses of constructions (as evidenced, e.g., by lexical preferences for verbs that fit the prototypical semantics of a construction). From a usage-based perspective (Bybee 2010), this makes perfect sense: in later stages, an emerging variety is used by more speakers and in more domains. As a result, more input for the pattern will be available, leading in turn to greater productivity.

It is important to point out, however, that this quantitative hypothesis does not deny the importance of qualitative innovations at all phases of the Dynamic Model (e.g., new complementation patterns such as *resemble to s.o.* instead of *resemble s.o.* in Singapore English, *pick s.o.* instead of *pick s.o. up* in East African English, Fiji English and Singapore English or *protest sth.* instead of *protest against sth.* in New Zealand English; cf. Schneider 2007: 46–783). This is also true for more abstract constructions. For the Comparative Correlative construction, Hoffmann (2014, 2019) found first evidence for meso-constructions that are qualitatively different from Standard English CCs, such as Kenyan English: *as the hours are reduced **the less** the salary will be* (ICE-KenE: soc-letk) or Jamaican English: *as more fatty deposits form on the arterial walls, **the more** difficult it is for the fat molecules to pass through the tiny capillaries . . .* (ICE-JA: W2B-022), in which the first clause C1 is realized as an *as*-clause, while the second C2 exhibits the expected British English comparative correlative pattern (cf. ***the more** the hours are reduced **the less** the salary will be* or ***the more** fatty deposits form on the arterial walls, **the more** difficult it is for the fat molecules to pass through the tiny capillaries . . .*). In these tokens, speakers have creatively adjusted the comparative correlative pattern in a way that emphasizes the semantic subordination of C1 as the protasis/independent variable to the apodosis/dependent variable C2 (and minimized the parallel semantic clause-internal computation that seems to influence the syntactic form of Standard British and American English CCs; for details see Hoffmann 2019). In contrast to Standard British and American English CCs, in which the parallel syntax of C1 and C2 mirrors their parallel computation of the two clauses (with something increasing or decreasing over a specified time span), it is expected that such innovations in New Englishes will highlight the asymmetric protasis–apodosis relationship of the two clauses. The degree to which such asymmetric new construction templates arise will, however, also depend on potential L1 transfer effects (i.e., the issue of how comparative correlative meanings are expressed by the local L1 languages and whether these exhibit more symmetric or asymmetric CC constructions). In any case, in line with my predictions, any type of innovative constructions should be more item-based in Phase III varieties, and should display more lexical variation in their constructional slots in Phase IV and Phase V varieties.

Finally, while I expect Phase V varieties to share a high productivity of constructional patterns, that does not mean that varieties at this stage will necessarily share the same types of lexical fillers for slots. Instead, as predicted by the Dynamic Model, varieties at later stages will diverge qualitatively not only from the former colonial model (British English), but also from each other.

The constructionist approach presented in this paper is not intended to supersede more qualitative or sociolinguistic work on post-colonial Englishes. Instead, as I hope to have shown, its cognitive nature is intended to complement the rich sociolinguistic Dynamic Model. What Construction Grammar brings to the Dynamic Model is a cognitive theory that generates predictions that can be tested empirically, such as the Dynamic Model Productivity hypothesis (something that Gries, Bernaisch and Heller (2018) vehemently argue for). In addition to this quantitative hypothesis, these predictions are also qualitative in nature: during the genesis of pidgins, for example, input frequency plays a role, but due to the limited use of these varieties, domain-general processes (such as analogical or metaphorical thinking) are expected to assume even greater importance. Moreover, as recent cognitive sociolinguistic studies (e.g., Hoffmann 2015; Hoffmann 2022: chapter 6; Hollmann 2013) have illustrated, constructionist approaches can also be used successfully to analyze the active stylization of individuals through dynamic acts of identity (the focus of third wave sociolinguistics and a phenomenon that Hundt (2020) points out should be given more attention in World Englishes studies).

Language is both a social and a cognitive phenomenon. What Construction Grammar offers to World Englishes studies is a full-fledged theoretical framework that is highly compatible with sociolinguistic approaches to language, variation and change. Together with the Dynamic Model, it, therefore, has the potential to considerably further our understanding of the genesis and evolution of New Englishes and to generate new and exciting fields of World Englishes research.

References

Allen, Kachina, Francisco Pereira, Matthew Botvinick and Adele E. Goldberg. 2012. Distinguishing grammatical constructions with fMRI pattern analysis. *Brain and Language* 123(3): 174–82.

Baayen, R. Harald. 2001. *Word Frequency Distributions*. Dordrecht: Kluwer.

Baayen, R. Harald. 2008. *Analyzing Linguistic Variation: A Practical Introduction to Statistics Using R*. Cambridge: Cambridge University Press.

Baayen, R. Harald. 2009. Corpus linguistics in morphology: Morphological productivity. In Anke Lüdeling and Merja Kytö, eds. *Corpus Linguistics: An International Handbook*, Vol. 2. Berlin: De Gruyter, 899–919.

Baker, Paul and Magnus Huber. 2000. Constructing new pronominal systems from the Atlantic to the Pacific. In Jacques Arends, ed. Special Issue. *Creoles, Pidgins, and Sundry Languages: Essays in Honor of Pieter Seuren. Linguistics* 38(5): 833–66.

Barlow, Michael and Suzanne Kemmer, eds. 2000. *Usage-based Models of Language*. Stanford, CA: CSLI Publications.

Baroni, Marco and Stefan Evert. 2014. The zipfR package for lexical statistics: A tutorial introduction. 3 October 2014. zipfR version 0.6–7. http://zipfr .r-forge.r-project.org/materials/zipfr-tutorial.pdf (last accessed 8 October 2018).

Barðdal, Johanna. 2008. *Productivity: Evidence from Case and Argument Structure in Icelandic*, Constructional Approaches to Language 8. Amsterdam: John Benjamins.

Barðdal, Johanna. 2011. Lexical vs. structural case: A false dichotomy. *Morphology* 21(1): 619–54.

Bauer, Laurie. 2001. *Morphological Productivity*. Cambridge: Cambridge University Press.

Bencini, Giulia M. L. 2013. Psycholinguistics. In Thomas Hoffmann and Graeme Trousdale, eds. *The Oxford Handbook of Construction Grammar*. Oxford: Oxford University Press, 379–96.

Bencini, Giulia M. L. and Adele E. Goldberg. 2000. The contribution of Argument Structure Constructions to sentence meaning. *Journal of Memory and Language* 43: 640–51.

Bencini, Giulia M. L. and Virginia Valian. 2008. Abstract sentence representations in 3-year-olds: Evidence from comprehension and production. *Journal of Memory and Language* 59: 97–113.

Biber, Douglas, Stig Johansson, Geoffrey Leech, Susan Conrad and Edward Finegan. 1999. *Longman Grammar of Spoken and Written English.* Harlow: Longman.

Bickerton, Derek. 1981. *Roots of Language.* Ann Arbor, MI: Karoma Publishers.

Bickerton, Derek. 1984. The language bioprogram hypothesis. *The Behavioral and Brain Sciences* 7(2): 173–221.

Bickerton, Derek. 2008. *Bastard Tongues: A Trailblazing Linguist Finds Clues to our Common Humanity in the World's Lowliest Languages.* New York: Hill & Wang.

Blumenthal-Dramé, Alice. 2012. *Entrenchment in Usage-Based Theories: What Corpus Data Do and Do Not Reveal about the Mind.* Berlin: De Gruyter Mouton.

Blumenthal-Dramé, Alice. 2017. Entrenchment from a psycholinguistic and neurolinguistic perspective. In Hans-Jörg Schmid, ed. *Entrenchment and the Psychology of Language Learning: How We Reorganize and Adapt Linguistic Knowledge.* Berlin: De Gruyter, 129–52.

Boas, Hans C. 2005. Determining the productivity of Resultative Constructions: A reply to Goldberg & Jackendoff. *Language* 81(2): 448–64.

Boas, Hans C. 2011. Zum Abstraktionsgrad von Resultativkonstruktionen. In Stefan Engelberg, Kristel Proost and Anke Holler, eds. *Sprachliches Wissen zwischen Lexikon und Grammatik.* Berlin/New York: De Gruyter, 37–69.

Boas, Hans C. 2013. Cognitive Construction Grammar. In Thomas Hoffmann and Graeme Trousdale, eds. *The Oxford Handbook of Construction Grammar.* Oxford: Oxford University Press, 233–52.

Boas, Hans C. and Ryan Dux. 2017. From the past into the present: From case frames to semantic frames. *Linguistics Vanguard* 3(1): 1–14.

Borlongan, Ariane Macalinga. 2016. Relocating Philippine English in Schneider's dynamic model. *Asian Englishes* 18(3): 232–41.

Brooks, Patricia and Michael Tomasello. 1999a. Young children learn to produce passives with nonce verbs. *Developmental Psychology* 35: 29–44.

Brooks, Patricia and Michael Tomasello. 1999b. How children constrain their Argument Structure Constructions. *Language* 75: 720–38.

Brooks, Patricia, Michael Tomasello, Kelly Dodson and Lawrence B. Lewis. 1999. Young children's overgeneralizations with fixed transitivity verbs. *Child Development* 70: 1325–37.

Bruckmaier, Elisabeth. 2017. *Getting at Get in World Englishes. A Corpus-Based Semasiological-Syntactic Analysis.* Berlin: De Gruyter.

Brunner, Thomas and Thomas Hoffmann. 2020. The *way* construction in World Englishes. *English World-Wide* 41(1): 1–32.

Buschfeld, Sarah, Thomas Hoffmann, Magnus Huber and Alexander Kautzsch. 2014. The evolution of Englishes: The dynamic model and beyond. In Sarah Buschfeld, Thomas Hoffmann, Magnus Huber and Alexander Kautzsch, eds. *The Evolution of Englishes*, Varieties of English Around the World G49. Amsterdam: John Benjamins, 1–17.

Buschfeld, Sarah and Alexander Kautzsch. 2017. Towards an integrated approach to postcolonial and non-postcolonial Englishes. *World Englishes* 36(1): 104–26.

Buschfeld, Sarah and Alexander Kautzsch. 2020. Theoretical models of English as a world language. In Daniel Schreier, Marianne Hundt and Edgar W. Schneider, eds. *Cambridge Handbook of World Englishes*. Cambridge: Cambridge University Press, 51–71.

Buschfeld, Sarah and Edgar W. Schneider. 2020. World Englishes: Postcolonial Englishes and beyond. In Ee Ling Low and Anne Pakir, eds. *World Englishes: Re-Thinking Paradigms*. London: Routledge, 29–46.

Bybee, Joan L. 1985. *Morphology: A Study into the Relation between Meaning and Form*. Amsterdam: John Benjamins.

Bybee, Joan L. 1995. Regular morphology and the lexicon. *Language and Cognitive Processes* 10: 425–55.

Bybee, Joan L. 2006. From usage to grammar: The mind's response to repetition. *Language* 82: 711–33.

Bybee, Joan L. 2010. *Language, Usage and Cognition*. Cambridge: Cambridge University Press.

Bybee, Joan L. 2013. Usage-based theory and exemplar representations of constructions. In Thomas Hoffmann and Graeme Trousdale, eds. *The Oxford Handbook of Construction Grammar*. Oxford: Oxford University Press, 49–69.

Cappelle, Bert, Yury Shtyrov and Friedemann Pulvermüller. 2010. Heating up or cooling up the brain? MEG evidence that phrasal verbs are lexical units. *Brain and Language* 115(3): 189–201.

Chang, Franklin. 2002. Symbolically speaking: A connectionist model of sentence production. *Cognitive Science* 26: 609–51.

Chang, Franklin, J. Kathryn Bock and Adele E. Goldberg. 2003. Can thematic roles leave traces of their places? *Cognition* 90: 29–49.

Chang, Franklin, Gary S. Dell, J. Kathryn Bock and Zenzi M. Griffin. 2000. Structural priming as implicit learning: A comparison of models of sentence production. *Journal of Psycholinguistic Research* 29: 217–29.

Chomsky, Noam. 1995. *The Minimalist Program*. Cambridge, MA: The MIT Press.

Chomsky, Noam. 2001. Derivation by phase. In Michael Kenstowicz, ed. *Ken Hale: A Life in Language*. Cambridge, MA: The MIT Press, 1–52.

Clark, Eve V. 1987. The principle of contrast: A constraint on language acquisition. In Brian MacWhinney, ed. *Mechanisms of Language Acquisition*. Hillsdale, NJ: Erlbaum, 1–33.

Croft, William. 2001. *Radical Construction Grammar*. Oxford: Oxford University Press.

Croft, William. 2012. *Verbs: Aspect and Causal Structure*. Oxford: Oxford University Press.

Croft, William and Alan D. Cruse. 2004. *Cognitive Linguistics*. Cambridge: Cambridge University Press.

Crystal, David. 2003. *English as a Global Language*, 2nd ed. Cambridge: Cambridge University Press.

Crystal, David. 2008. Two thousand million? *English Today* 24: 3–6. http://doi .org/10.1017/S0266078408000023.

Dąbrowska, Eva. 2000. From formula to schema: The acquisition of English questions. *Cognitive Linguistics* 11: 83–102.

Dąbrowska, Eva and Elena Lieven. 2005. Towards a lexically specific grammar of children's question constructions. *Cognitive Linguistics* 16: 437–74.

Dąbrowska, Eva, Caroline Rowland and Anna Theakston. 2009. The acquisition of questions with long-distance dependencies. *Cognitive Linguistics* 20: 571–98.

Dancygier, Barbara. 2017. Cognitive linguistics and the study of textual meaning. In Barbara Dancygier, ed. *The Cambridge Handbook of Cognitive Linguistics*. Cambridge: Cambridge University Press, 607–22.

Desagulier, Guillaume. 2016. A lesson from associative learning: Asymmetry and productivity in multiple-slot constructions. *Corpus Linguistics and Linguistic Theory* 12(2): 173–219.

Diessel, Holger. 2004. *The Acquisition of Complex Sentences*. Cambridge: Cambridge University Press.

Diessel, Holger. 2005. Competing motivations for the ordering of main and adverbial clauses. *Linguistics* 43(3): 449–79.

Diessel, Holger. 2009. On the role of frequency and similarity in the acquisition of subject and non-subject relative clauses. In Talmy Givón and Masayoshi Shibatani, eds. *Syntactic Complexity*. Amsterdam: John Benjamins, 251–76.

Diessel, Holger. 2013. Construction Grammar and first language acquisition. In Thomas Hoffmann and Graeme Trousdale, eds. *The Oxford Handbook of Construction Grammar*. Oxford: Oxford University Press, 347–78.

Dominey, Peter and Michael Hoen. 2006. Structure mapping and semantic integration in a construction-based neurolinguistic model of sentence processing. *Cortex* 42: 476–79.

Ellis, Nick C. 2002. Frequency effects in language processing: A review with implications for theories of implicit and explicit language acquisition. *Studies in Second Language Acquisition* 24(2): 143–88.

Ellis, Nick C. 2003. Constructions, chunking and connectionism: The emergence of second language structure. In Catherine Doughty and Michael H. Long, eds. *Handbook of Second Language Acquisition*. Oxford: Blackwell, 63–103.

Ellis, Nick C. 2006. Cognitive perspectives on SLA: The associative cognitive CREED. *AILA Review* 19: 100–21.

Ellis, Nick C. 2013. Construction Grammar and second language acquisition. In Thomas Hoffmann and Graeme Trousdale, eds. *The Oxford Handbook of Construction Grammar*. Oxford: Oxford University Press, 365–78.

Ellis, Nick C. and Fernando Ferreira-Junior. 2009. Constructions and their acquisition: Islands and the distinctiveness of their occupancy. *Annual Review of Cognitive Linguistics* 7: 188–221.

Evans, Stephan. 2009. The evolution of the English-language speech community in Hong Kong. *English World-Wide* 30(3): 278–301.

Evert, Stefan. 2004. A simple LNRE model for random character sequences. *Proceedings of JADT 2004*, 411–22.

Evert, Stefan and Marco Baroni. 2007. *zipfR*: Word frequency distributions in R. *Proceedings of the 45th Annual Meeting of the Association for Computational Linguistics, Posters and Demonstrations Sessions*, 29–32.

Fillmore, Charles J. 1977. Scenes-and-frames semantics. In Antonio Zampolli, ed. *Linguistics Structures Processing*. Amsterdam: North Holland Publishing Company, 55–81.

Fillmore, Charles J. 1982. Frame semantics. In The Linguistic Society of Korea, ed. *Linguistics in the Morning Calm*. Seoul: Hanshin, 111–37.

Fillmore, Charles J. 1985. Frames and the semantics of understanding. *Quaderni di Semantica* 6(2): 222–54.

Fillmore, Charles J. 2006. Frames semantics. In Keith Brown, ed. *Encyclopedia of Linguistics and Language*, Vol. 4. Amsterdam: Elsevier, 613–20.

Fillmore, Charles J. and Collin F. Baker. 2010. A frames approach to semantic analysis. In Bernd Heine and Heiko Narrog, eds. *The Oxford Handbook of Linguistic Analysis*. Oxford: Oxford University Press, 313–39.

Givón, Talmy. 1985. Iconicity, isomorphism and non-arbitrary coding in syntax. In John Haiman, ed. *Iconicity in Syntax*. Amsterdam: John Benjamins, 187–219.

Goldberg, Adele E. 1995. *Constructions: A Construction Grammar Approach to Argument Structure*. Chicago: University of Chicago Press.

Goldberg, Adele E. 2006. *Constructions at Work: The Nature of Generalization in Language*. Oxford: Oxford University Press.

Goldberg, Adele E. 2019. *Explain Me This: Creativity, Competition and the Partial Pproductivity of Constructions*. Princeton, NJ: Princeton University Press.

Goldberg, Adele E. and Ray Jackendoff. 2004. The English resultative as a family of constructions. *Language* 80: 532–68.

Gries, Stefan Th. 2004. *HCFA 3.2 – A Program for Hierarchical Configural Frequency Analysis for R for Windows*. www.linguistics.ucsb.edu/people/ stefan-th-gries (program available on request; last accessed 8 April 2018).

Gries, Stefan Th. 2009. *Statistics for Linguistics with R: A Practical Introduction*. Berlin: De Gruyter Mouton.

Gries, Stefan Th. 2013. Data in Construction Grammar. In Thomas Hoffmann and Graeme Trousdale, eds. *The Oxford Handbook of Construction Grammar*. Oxford: Oxford University Press, 93–108.

Gries, Stefan Th., Tobias Bernaisch and Benedikt Heller. 2018. A corpus-linguistic account of the history of the genitive alternation in Singapore English. In Sandra C. Deshors, ed. *Modelling World Englishes: Assessing the Interplay of Emancipation and Globalization of ESL Varieties*. Amsterdam: John Benjamins, 245–79.

Gries, Stefan Th., Beate Hampe and Doris Schönefeld. 2005. Converging evidence: Bringing together experimental and corpus data on the association of verbs and constructions. *Cognitive Linguistics* 16: 635–76.

Gries, Stefan Th., Beate Hampe and Doris Schönefeld. 2010. Converging evidence II: More on the association of verbs and constructions. In Sally Rice and John Newman, eds. *Empirical and Experimental Methods in Cognitive/Functional Research*. Stanford, CA: CSLI, 59–72.

Gries, Stefan Th. and Stefanie Wulff. 2005. Do foreign language learners also have constructions? Evidence from priming, sorting and corpora. *Annual Review of Cognitive Linguistics* 3: 182–200.

Gries, Stefan Th. and Stefanie Wulff. 2009. Psycholinguistic and corpus-linguistic evidence for L2 constructions. *Annual Review of Cognitive Linguistics* 7(1): 163–86.

Haïk, Isabelle. 2012. *The hell* in English grammar. In Nicole Le Querler, Franck Neveu and Emmanuelle Roussel, eds. *Relations, Connexions, Dépendances: Hommage au Professeur Claude Guimier*. Rennes: Presses Universitaires de Rennes, 101–26.

Haiman, John. 1980. The iconicity of grammar: Isomorphism and motivation. *Language* 56(3): 515–40.

Haiman, John. 1983. Iconic and economic motivation. *Language* 59(4): 781–819.

Haiman, John. 1985. *Natural Syntax*. Cambridge: Cambridge University Press.

Hilpert, Martin. 2013. *Constructional Change in English: Developments in Allomorphy, Word Formation, and Syntax*. Cambridge: Cambridge University Press.

Hilpert, Martin. 2019. *Construction Grammar and Its Application to English*, 2nd ed. Edinburgh: Edinburgh University Press.

Hoeksema, Jack and Donna J. Napoli. 2008. Just for the hell of it: A comparison of two taboo-term constructions. *Journal of Linguistics* 44 (2): 347–78.

Hoffmann, Thomas. 2011. *Preposition Placement in English: A Usage-based Approach*. Cambridge: Cambridge University Press.

Hoffmann, Thomas. 2014. The cognitive evolution of Englishes: The role of constructions in the Dynamic Model. In Sarah Buschfeld, Thomas Hoffmann, Magnus Huber and Alexander Kautzsch, eds. *The Evolution of Englishes: The Dynamic Model and Beyond*, Varieties of English Around the World G49. Amsterdam: John Benjamins, 160–80.

Hoffmann, Thomas. 2015. Cognitive sociolinguistic aspects of football chants: The role of social and physical context in usage-based Construction Grammar. *Zeitschrift für Anglistik und Amerikanistik* 63(3): 273–94.

Hoffmann, Thomas. 2017a. From constructions to Construction Grammars. In Barbara Dancygier, ed. *The Cambridge Handbook of Cognitive Linguistics*, 284–309. Cambridge: Cambridge University Press.

Hoffmann, Thomas. 2017b. Construction Grammars. In Barbara Dancygier, ed. *The Cambridge Handbook of Cognitive Linguistics*. Cambridge: Cambridge University Press, 310–29.

Hoffmann, Thomas. 2019. *English Comparative Correlatives: Diachronic and Synchronic Variation at the Lexicon-Syntax Interface*. Cambridge: Cambridge University Press.

Hoffmann, Thomas. 2020. Marginal Argument Structure constructions: The [V *the* Ntaboo-word *out of*]-construction in post-colonial Englishes. *Linguistics Vanguard* 6.

Hoffmann, Thomas. 2022. *Construction Grammar: The Structure of English*, Cambridge Textbooks in Linguistics. Cambridge: Cambridge University Press.

Hoffmann, Thomas and Graeme Trousdale, eds. 2013. *The Oxford Handbook of Construction Grammar*. Oxford: Oxford University Press.

Hollmann, Willem. 2013. Constructions in cognitive sociolinguistics. In Thomas Hoffmann and Graeme Trousdale, eds. *The Oxford Handbook of Construction Grammar*. Oxford: Oxford University Press, 491–509.

Hundt, Marianne. 2020. On models and modelling. *World Englishes* 1–20.

Johnson, Matt A. and Adele E. Goldberg. 2013. Evidence for automatic accessing of constructional meaning: Jabberwocky sentences prime associated verbs. *Language and Cognitive Processes* 28(10): 1439–52.

Kachru, Braj B., ed. 1992. *The Other Tongue: English Across Cultures*, 2nd ed. Urbana, IL: University of Illinois Press.

Konopka, Agnieszka E. and Kathryn Bock. 2008. Lexical or syntactic control of sentence formulation? Structural generalizations from idiom production. *Cognitive Psychology* 58: 68–101.

Langacker, Ronald W. 1991. *Foundations of Cognitive Grammar*, Vol. 2. Stanford, CA: Stanford University Press.

Lange, Matthew K. 2004. British colonial legacies and political development. *World Development* 32(6): 905–22.

Laporte, Samantha. 2019. The patterning of the high-frequency verb make in varieties of English: A Construction Grammar approach. PhD thesis, Catholic University: Louvain-la-Neuve.

Lefebvre, Claire. 2004. *Issues in the Study of Pidgin and Creole Languages*, Studies in Language Companion Series 70. Amsterdam: John Benjamins.

Le Page, R. B. and Andrée Tabouret-Keller. 1985. *Acts of Identity: Creole-based Approaches to Language and Ethnicity*. Cambridge: Cambridge University Press.

Martin, Isabel Pefianco. 2014. Beyond nativization? Philippine English in Schneider's Dynamic Model. In Sarah Buschfeld, Thomas Hoffmann, Magnus Huber and Alexander Kautzsch, eds. *The Evolution of Englishes: The Dynamic Model and Beyond*, Varieties of English Around the World G49. Amsterdam: John Benjamins, 70–85.

McDonough, Kim. 2006. Interaction and syntactic priming: English L2 speakers' production of Dative Constructions. *Studies in Second Language Acquisition* 28: 179–207.

McDonough, Kim and Alison Mackey. 2006. Responses to recasts: Repetitions, primed production and linguistic development. *Language Learning* 56: 693–720.

McDonough, Kim and Pavel Trofimovich. 2008. *Using Priming Methods in Second Language Research*. London: Routledge.

Mesthrie, Rajend. 2010. Socio-phonetics and social change: Deracialisation of the GOOSE vowel in South African English. *Journal of Sociolinguistics* 14 (1): 3–33.

Mesthrie, Rajend. 2014. The sociophonetic effects of 'Event X': Post-apartheid Black South African English in multicultural contact with other South African Englishes. In Sarah Buschfeld, Thomas Hoffmann, Magnus Huber and Alexander Kautzsch, eds. *The Evolution of Englishes: The Dynamic*

Model and Beyond, Varieties of English Around the World G49. Amsterdam: John Benjamins, 58–69.

Mesthrie, Rajend and Rakesh M. Bhatt. 2008. *World Englishes: The Study of New Linguistic Varieties*, Key Topics in Sociolinguistics. Cambridge: Cambridge University Press.

Mesthrie, Rajend, Joan Swann, Ana Deumert and William L. Leap. 2000. *Introducing Sociolinguistics*. Edinburgh: Edinburgh University Press.

Mufwene, Salikoko. 2001. *The Ecology of Language Evolution*. Cambridge: Cambridge University Press.

Mufwene, Salikoko. 2004. Language birth and death. *Annual Review of Anthropology* 33: 201–22.

Mukherjee, Joybrato. 2007. Steady states in the evolution of New Englishes: Present-day Indian English as an equilibrium. *Journal of English Linguistics* 35(2): 157–87.

Mukherjee, Joybrato and Stefan Th. Gries. 2009. Collostructional nativisation in New Englishes: Verb-construction associations in the International Corpus of English. *English World-Wide* 30(1): 27–51.

Nelson, Gerald, Sean Wallis and Bas Aarts. 2002. *Exploring Natural Language: Working with the British Component of the International Corpus of English*. Amsterdam: John Benjamins.

Patrick, Peter L. 2008. Jamaican Creole: Morphology and syntax. In Edgar W. Schneider, ed. *Varieties of English 2: The Americas and the Caribbean*. Berlin: De Gruyter Mouton, 609–43.

Perek, Florent. 2015. *Argument Structure in Usage-based Construction Grammar*, Constructional Approaches to Language 17. Amsterdam: John Benjamins.

Perek, Florent. 2016. Using distributional semantics to study syntactic productivity in diachrony: A case study. *Linguistics* 54(1): 149–88.

Plag, Ingo. 2003. *Word-Formation in English*. Cambridge: Cambridge University Press.

Plag, Ingo. 2006. Productivity. In Bas Aarts and April M. S. McMahon, eds. *The Handbook of English Linguistics*. Malden: Blackwell, 537–56.

Pulvermüller, Friedemann. 1993. On connecting syntax and the brain. In Ad Aertsen, ed. *Brain Theory: Spatio-temporal Aspects of Brain Function*. New York: Elsevier, 131–45.

Pulvermüller, Friedemann. 2003. *The Neuroscience of Language*. Cambridge: Cambridge University Press.

Pulvermüller, Friedemann. 2010. Brain embodiment of syntax and grammar: Discrete combinatorial mechanisms spelt out in neuronal circuits. *Brain and Language* 112(3): 167–79.

Pulvermüller, Friedemann, Bert Cappelle and Yury Shtyrov. 2013. Brain basis of meaning, words, constructions, and grammar. In Thomas Hoffmann and Graeme Trousdale, eds. *The Oxford Handbook of Construction Grammar*. Oxford: Oxford University Press, 397–416.

Pulvermüller, Friedemann and Andreas Knoblauch. 2009. Discrete combinatorial circuits emerging in neural networks: A mechanism for rules of grammar in the human brain? *Neural Networks* 22(2): 161–72.

Quirk, Randolph. 1985. The English language in a global context. In Randolph Quirk and Henry G. Widdowson, eds., *English in the World: Teaching and Learning the Language and Literatures*. Cambridge: Cambridge University Press, 1–6.

Quirk, Randolph, Sidney Greenbaum, Geoffrey Leech and Jan Svartvik. 1985. *A Comprehensive Grammar of the English Language*. London: Longman.

Rowland, Caroline F. 2007. Explaining errors in children's questions. *Cognition* 104: 106–34.

Rowland, Caroline F. and Julian M. Pine. 2000. Subject-auxiliary inversion errors and wh-question acquisition: What children do know? *Journal of Child Language* 27: 157–81.

Schmid, Hans-Jörg. 2016. *English Morphology and Word-Formation: An Introduction*, 3rd ed. Berlin: Erich Schmidt.

Schmid, Hans-Jörg. 2020 *The Dynamics of the Linguistic System. Usage, Conventionalization, and Entrenchment*. Oxford: Oxford University Press.

Schneider, Edgar W. 2003. The dynamics of New Englishes: From identity construction to dialect birth. *Language* 79(2): 233–81.

Schneider, Edgar W. 2007. *Postcolonial English: Varieties Around the World*. Cambridge: Cambridge University Press.

Schneider, Edgar W. 2012. Exploring the interface between World Englishes and Second Language Acquisition – and implications for English as a Lingua Franca. *Journal of English as a Lingua Franca* 1(1): 57–91.

Schneider, Edgar W. 2020. *English Around the World*, 2nd ed., Cambridge Introductions to the English Language. Cambridge: Cambridge University Press.

Stefanowitsch, Anatol and Susanne Flach. 2017. The corpus-based perspective on entrenchment. In Hans-Jörg Schmid, ed. *Entrenchment and the Psychology of Language learning: How We Reorganize and Adapt Linguistic Knowledge*. Berlin: De Gruyter, 101–27.

Steger, Maria and Schneider, Edgar W. 2012. Complexity as a function of iconicity. In Bernd Kortmann and Benedikt Szmrecsanyi, eds. *Linguistic Complexity: Second Language Acquisition, Indigenization, Contact*. Berlin: De Gruyter, 156–91.

Szmrecsanyi, Benedikt and Bernd Kortmann. 2009. Between simplification and complexification: Nonstandard varieties of English around the world. In Geoffrey Sampson, David Gil and Peter Trudgill, eds. *Language Complexity as an Evolving Variable*. Oxford: Oxford University Press, 64–79.

Thomason, Sarah G. 2001. *Language Contact: An Introduction*. Washington, DC: Georgetown University Press.

Thusat, Joshua, Emily Anderson, Shante Davis et al. 2009. Maltese English and the nativization phase of the dynamic model. *English Today* 97 25, 2: 25–32.

Tomasello, Michael. 1992. *First Verbs: A Case Study of Early Grammatical Development*. Cambridge: Cambridge University Press.

Tomasello, Michael. 1999. *The Cultural Origins of Human Cognition: An Essay*. Cambridge, MA: Harvard University Press.

Tomasello, Michael. 2003. *Constructing a Language: A Usage-based Theory of Language Acquisition*. Cambridge, MA: Harvard University Press.

Tomasello, Michael. 2006. Construction Grammar for kids. *Constructions* Special Volume 1. www.constructions-journal.com.

Tomasello, Michael and Patricia Brooks. 1998. Young children's earliest Transitive and Intransitive Constructions. *Cognitive Linguistics* 9: 379–95.

Traugott, Elizabeth and Graeme Trousdale. 2013. *Constructionalization and Constructional Changes*, Oxford Studies in Diachronic and Historical Linguistics. Oxford: Oxford University Press.

Trudgill, Peter. 2004. *New-Dialect Formation: The Inevitability of Colonial Englishes*. Edinburgh: Edinburgh University Press.

Van Rooy, Bertus. 2010. Social and linguistic perspectives on variability in World Englishes. *World Englishes* 29(1): 3–20.

Van Rooy, Bertus. 2014. Convergence and endonormativity at phase 4 of the Dynamic Model. In Sarah Buschfeld, Thomas Hoffmann, Magnus Huber and Alexander Kautzsch, eds. *The Evolution of Englishes: The Dynamic Model and Beyond*, Varieties of English Around the World G49. Amsterdam: John Benjamins, 21–38.

Veale, Tony. 2012. *Exploding the Creativity Myth: The Computational Foundations of Linguistic Creativity*. London: Bloomsbury.

Velupillai, Viveka. 2015. *Pidgins, Creoles and Mixed Languages: An Introduction*. Amsterdam: John Benjamins.

Wardlow Lane, Liane and Victor S. Ferreira. 2010. Abstract syntax in sentence production: Evidence from stem-exchange errors. *Journal of Memory and Language* 62: 151–65.

Weston, Daniel. 2011. Gibraltar's position in the dynamic model of postcolonial English. *English World-Wide* 32(3): 338–67.

Wiechmann, Daniel. 2008. On the computation of collostruction strength: Testing measures of association as expressions of lexical bias. *Corpus Linguistics and Linguistic Theory* 4: 253–90.

Winford, Donald. 2003. *An Introduction to Contact Linguistics*. Malden, MA: Blackwell.

Wulff, Stefanie, Nick C. Ellis, Ute Römer et al. 2009. The acquisition of tense-aspect: Converging evidence from corpora, cognition and learner constructions. *Modern Language Journal* 93: 354–69.

Zeldes, Amir. 2013. Productive argument selection: Is lexical semantics enough? *Corpus Linguistics and Linguistic Theory* 9(2): 263–91.

Ziegler, Jayden, Giulia Bencini, Adele Goldberg and Jesse Snedeker. 2019. How abstract is syntax? Evidence from structural priming. *Cognition* 193: 104045.

Cambridge Elements $\equiv$

World Englishes

Edgar W. Schneider
University of Regensburg
Edgar W. Schneider is Professor Emeritus of English Linguistics at the University of Regensburg, Germany. His many books include *Postcolonial English* (Cambridge, 2007), *English around the World, 2e* (Cambridge, 2020) and *The Cambridge Handbook of World Englishes* (Cambridge, 2020).

About the Series
Over the last centuries, the English language has spread all over the globe due to a multitude of factors including colonization and globalization. In investigating these phenomena, the vibrant linguistic sub-discipline of "World Englishes" has grown substantially, developing appropriate theoretical frameworks and considering applied issues. This Elements series will cover all the topics of the discipline in an accessible fashion and will be supplemented by on-line material.

Cambridge Elements $^{\equiv}$

World Englishes

Elements in the Series

Uniformity and Variability in the Indian English Accent
Caroline R. Wiltshire

Posthumanist World Englishes
Lionel Wee

The Cognitive Foundation of Post-colonial Englishes: Construction Grammar as the Cognitive Theory for the Dynamic Model
Thomas Hoffmann

Printed in the United States
by Baker & Taylor Publisher Services

Printed in the United States
by Baker & Taylor Publisher Services